Stewart Whyte is a world-leading authority on how to set up and run B&Bs and other types of small accommodation businesses. In 2007 Stewart wrote the curriculum for two online courses for the Bed & Breakfast Institute, which is currently marketed in seven countries. He lectures regularly on the subject and is the author of thirteen books on how to get into the B&B industry. As well as having first-hand experience at running profitable B&Bs, Stewart has helped develop regional tourism strategies in many parts of the world.

Also available

How To Start & Run a B&B
Do It Yourself Bookkeeping for Small Businesses
Quick Wins in Sales and Marketing
The Small Business Start-up Workbook
Start and Run a Business from Home

Earn Money From Your Home

Stewart Whyte

··············

A How To Book

ROBINSON

ROBINSON

First published in Great Britain as *How To Start and Run a B&B 3rd edition* in 2011 by How To Books

This edition published in Great Britain in 2017 by Robinson

ISBN 978-1-47213-773-9

Typeset by Hewer Text UK Ltd, Edinburgh

Printed and bound in Great Britain by CPI Group (UK) Ltd, Croydon CR0 4YY

Robinson
An imprint of
Little, Brown Book Group
Carmelite House
50 Victoria Embankment
London EC4Y 0DZ

An Hachette UK Company
www.hachette.co.uk

www.littlebrown.co.uk

How To Books are published by Robinson, an imprint of Little, Brown Book Group. We welcome proposals from authors who have first-hand experience of their subjects. Please set out the aims of your book, its target market and its suggested contents in an email to Nikki.Read@howtobooks.co.uk

Contents

Preface **xi**
Acknowledgements **xiii**

CHAPTER 1   **The Sharing Economy** 1
Major Online Reservation Platforms Available 1
Deciding to Enter the Short-Let and
   B&B Market **2**
Market Options **4**
Short-Break Holidays **4**

CHAPTER 2   **Issues to Consider Before Taking the Plunge** 5
Why the B&B/Holiday-Let Industry is Becoming
   So Popular **5**
Deciding on the Location **5**
Computer Literacy **6**
Equal Commitment **6**

CHAPTER 3   **Defining Your Target Market** 9
Choosing the Type of Guest You Want
   to Attract **9**
The Corporate Market **10**
Single Travellers **11**
Women Travellers **11**
The Gay Market **11**
People With a Disability **11**
The Family Market **12**
No Smoking **12**
No Children **12**
No Pets **12**

CHAPTER 4   **Choosing and Preparing Your Property** 15

Using your Current Property **15**

Are You in the Right Location? **16**

Accessing Your Property for
Holiday-Let Potential **16**

Deciding Whether to Convert Your Current
Property or Buy or Build a New One **17**

Buying an Established Holiday Let/B&B **17**

Identifying Your Property **19**

Making a Good First Impression **19**

Your Entrance **20**

Living Rooms **21**

Dining Rooms **23**

The Kitchen **25**

Bathrooms and Toilets **26**

Bedrooms **29**

Home Office **31**

CHAPTER 5   **Viability and Local Bodies** 33

Deciding Whether Your Property is Viable **33**

Building and Development Applications **33**

Local Bodies, Holiday Lets and B&Bs **34**

Approval and Construction of Holiday
and B&B Accommodation **35**

Fire Safety **36**

Planning Permission **38**

CHAPTER 6   **Planning for Success** 41

Being Prepared **41**

Financing Your Venture **43**

Using Your Business Plan **43**

Your Professional Support **43**

Your Accountant **44**

Your Solicitor **44**

Insurance **44**

B&B and Tourism Authorities **45**

A Good Business Mentor **45**

CHAPTER 7   **Hosting Issues to Consider 47**
Providing Information for Your
   Property Listing **47**
Features and Benefits **47**
Children, Pets or Smoking? **47**
Special Needs and Requirements **48**
Dietary Issues **48**
Local Activities and Attractions **48**
Deposits and Cancellations **48**
Behaviour **49**
Guest Behaviour **51**
Neighbours **51**
Complaints **52**
Follow-up **53**
The Importance of Feedback **53**
Safety Issues **54**
Making Your Holiday Let/B&B a Safe Place
   to Stay **54**
Making Your Holiday Let/B&B a Safe Place
   to Work **55**
Safety in the Kitchen **55**
Providing First Aid **56**

CHAPTER 8   **Food and the B&B 59**
The Full Cooked or Continental Breakfast **59**
The Breakfast Basket **60**
Offering Lunch **61**
Alcohol Licensing **61**
Morning Coffee and Afternoon Tea **61**
Eating With Guests **62**
Self-Contained Properties **62**
Knowing the Restaurants in Your Area **62**

CHAPTER 9   **Daily Operations 65**
Bookings **65**
Guest Registration **67**

Insurance **67**
Keeping Financial Records **70**
Housekeeping **71**
Being Prepared **72**
A Cleaning Checklist **72**
Taking Care of Your Furniture **72**

CHAPTER 10 **Joining the Hospitality Industry** **75**
The Structure of Tourism Authorities **75**
Local Tourist Organisations **76**
Bed and Breakfast Associations **76**
Destination Marketing **76**
Official Star Grading Definitions **77**
Statutory Obligations **77**
Grading **78**
Feasibility Study **79**
Creating a Financial Model **79**

CHAPTER 11 **Holiday Accommodation Marketing** **81**
Developing a Marketing Concept **81**
Doing Market Research **81**
Competition **83**
Records and Files **83**
Developing a Marketing Strategy **84**
Target Marketing **85**
The Marketing Mix **86**
Products and Services **86**
Promotion and Advertising **86**
Public Relations **87**
How Much Marketing Do I Need? **89**
Newsletters **91**

CHAPTER 12 **Online Reservation Platforms** **93**
How Online Reservation Platforms Work **93**

Online Reservation Platform Fees and
    Commission Structures **95**
How Do Airbnb References Work? **95**

CHAPTER 13 **Business Basics** 97
Choosing a Legal Structure **97**
Business Names **98**
Setting Your Room Rate **98**
Tax Obligations **99**
Smartphones **100**
The Internet **100**
Creating a Website **100**
Milestones **101**
Managing Customer Contact **102**

Epilogue: For the Future **105**
Index **107**

Preface

The growth of holiday let and Bed and Breakfast as an accommodation alternative is a remarkable recent success story in the Western world. Many people are choosing to list their home with the world's largest holiday online reservation platforms such as Airbnb, TripAdvisor, Wimdu and Expedia.

To meet demand and substantiate Bed and Breakfast's place in the accommodation industry there is a growing need for increased knowledge and professionalism among holiday let operators and, in particular, those people considering entry into this sector of tourism.

During the last five years the shared economy has taken off, with Airbnb, Wimdu and Uber leading the charge. These companies are all part of a revised industry that uses hi-tech websites and apps to promote shared assets and resources that enable the listed properties often to bypass local government rules and regulations that traditional operators have had to abide by.

As a point of interest, Bed and Breakfasts in most countries have to abide by local government rules and regulations, whereas the holiday let industry is not regulated to the same extent. This situation, however, is already changing.

The Shared Economy is here to stay, which is why Airbnb, TripAdvisor, Wimdu, Expedia and booking.com are so popular with the travelling public. They have a multi-million audience of tourists wanting to book accommodation.

Current trends show that changes in the workplace could be one of the main contributors to the high level of interest in becoming a Bed and Breakfast operator or listing a holiday let. Another influential factor is the growth of the short-break holiday market – a growth industry that promises to reach well into this century. Those who take short-break holidays, which often includes some time devoted to work, historically prefer this form of accommodation.

To make additional income from using your home is the dream of many potential readers. This book will give you the knowledge and confidence you need to turn your house into a holiday let or a B&B. It will help you to understand better the issues relating to responsible hosting and being a viable accommodation provider. It covers the following:

★ Getting your property ready for a successful listing.
★ Being a responsible host.
★ What is required to list your property on online reservation platforms, and how to do so.
★ How to make good money by listing your home.
★ Monitoring your bookings and how to set your room rate.
★ How to market your property internationally with very little capital outlay.

It is important to remember, however, that knowledge is not an end in itself. Use the knowledge gained from this publication as a resource and stepping stone to achieve your own goals and aspirations.

The main message is that the research you need to do to make your holiday let/B&B a success must be personal to you and your market.

All issues covered in this book are significant, but professionalism, both on your part and on the part of those who advise you, is the most important. This book will reinforce the need to seek professional advice in the early stages of your venture and give you an insight into the level of professionalism you need in order to make a success of this business.

Stewart

Acknowledgements

This book would not be as comprehensive as it is without the wonderful contribution of the following people and organisations: Gideon Stanley from Gracesoft for his reservation network insights, Warren Whyte for his advice on banking procedures; Ryan Insurance Group for their advice on business insurance for B&B operators; and Dr Rita Helling for her insights on dealing with guest issues.

I thank Suellen Harwood for her input and proofreading contribution.

I would like to thank all of the Holiday Let/B&B owners for their advice and anecdotes, which offer invaluable insight to all newcomers into the industry.

CHAPTER 1

The Sharing Economy

The sharing economy is here to stay! It has been around for a long time and applies particularly to the accommodation industry. It had its beginnings with home swapping, letting your property and house sharing, the British Isles being particularly known for this type of accommodation. There is a home on Dartmoor, in Devon, that has been operating as a B&B since the early 1800s. The sharing economy has grown substantially in the last five years, with the likes of Airbnb leading the charge.

·····················

It is estimated that Airbnb has in excess of one and a half million listed properties in over a hundred and ninety countries throughout the world, and these numbers are expected to increase substantially over this and the next decade. Airbnb currently processes tens of millions of room nights a year, according to Reuters.

MAJOR ONLINE RESERVATION PLATFORMS AVAILABLE

Major reservation platforms include, to name a few:

★ TripAdvisor, which is the world's largest travel site reaching 350 million unique monthly visitors. Access their site and you will find more than 290 million property reviews and opinions covering more than 5.3 million accommodations, restaurants and attractions. As with other sites, these reviews are supplied by the travelling public. The site operates in forty-seven countries worldwide.

★ Wimdu is another reservation platform, with 300,000 apartments and holiday homes worldwide, including Bed and Breakfasts.

- ★ Expedia is another site with a directory of more than 80,000 accommodation properties worldwide and 4 million rooms, which includes Bed and Breakfasts.
- ★ Booking.com has more than 46,000 Bed and Breakfasts listed, as well as some other forms of accommodation.
- ★ Onefinestay: Tourism's new frontier? It might just be your home.

Most reservation platforms list holiday lets under the Bed and Breakfast category. It is up to the researcher to differentiate the type of property they require.

DECIDING TO ENTER THE SHORT-LET AND B&B MARKET

Making money from letting your property to the short-break market, and occasionally the long-term market, is a growth industry that promises to reach well into this century. Keep in mind that some clients require longer stays while they find suitable permanent accommodation. Now consider the questions below:

1 So, you want to run a holiday let or a Bed & Breakfast! WHY? This is very possibly the most important question you will ask yourself as you read this book.

WHY? Is it because you can let your house/apartment out by listing with Airbnb/TripAdvisor and, having stayed in a few properties over the years, it seems a nice way to make extra money from your home? Is it because you want to earn enough money to cover your mortgage payments, or you talked about making a sea-change decision and moving out of the city? Is it because you think it will be a way to make your fortune? Would it be a short-term means of earning some extra income for a special event; e.g. an overseas trip you always wanted to take?

2 Do you want to manage your own bookings and/or use an online reservation platform? This will be determined by the length of time you wish to stay in the market and by how much time you wish to devote to this area.

It's also important to look at your market options. This is discussed in more detail further on.

There are many different reasons people enter the holiday let/B&B market, and you need to think clearly about why you wish to do so. Because, make no mistake, the difference between a good and bad holiday let is you, the host. Why you are embarking on this adventure matters, because you plan to succeed. You will need to create a feasibility study that will match the goals you have for your property. Be prepared to discover that running this form of accommodation may not achieve those goals for you.

Holiday lets, as opposed to the traditional Bed and Breakfast, include the following types of accommodation: self-contained houses and cottages, a cottage at the bottom of your garden, holiday homes and apartments in city areas.

It should be pointed out that very few holiday lets will support you in the first few years. If you start out with one guest bedroom then your earning capacity could be limited. This will also be the case if you over-invest.

The main reasons for failure are over-capitalising on the part of the owners, and the management process of the property itself. Burnout can also be a significant factor in the pursuit of a lifestyle change.

There is a difference between spending on preferable features, such as en-suites or a dedicated bathroom for each guest bedroom, which many guests see as a necessity, and filling your house with expensive antiques, which will not always make a guest decide to stay with you or to return.

A flair for redecorating does not necessarily make you a good host. Neither does enjoying entertaining friends and family. Running a B&B is a twenty-four-hour commitment, whereas a holiday let is less demanding as guests often do not stay in your home and there is an option not to provide breakfast. In a classic B&B, you need to be prepared to 'entertain' at all hours of the day and night, have your private life disturbed, and in some cases share your personal space with strangers. This can be difficult, but if you are to be a successful host the spirit of giving must be embraced twenty-four hours a day. Whether you are a B&B or a holiday let host, this spirit should inhabit every exchange, every phone call, every letter or email. To be a successful host you need to LOVE PEOPLE and be prepared to share your life and sometimes your home with them. However, never forget quality time for yourself and your family.

MARKET OPTIONS

Before deciding exactly whom you are going to target for your holiday let/B&B, it is a good idea to know something about tourism in your country. Tourism is one of the largest industries in the world and you want to get it right. Following travel trends is essential and they should be monitored on a regular basis.

SHORT-BREAK HOLIDAYS

The short-break market has become increasingly significant in recent years, with current tourism trends throughout the world moving in favour of one- to three-night breaks rather than fortnightly holidays.

Most tourists today who want a short-break holiday search for and book them by clicking onto the major online reservation platforms, and that is the main reason for listing your property with Airbnb, Wimdu, TripAdvisor, Expedia and others, as they are a prime source for bookings.

As the major reservation platforms have a global presence, your listing attracts both the domestic market and the international one.

These social trends have already changed the nature of tourism. All tourist authorities have their own websites where, to help you do your homework, you can gather meaningful information regarding trends should you be contemplating opening a B&B or providing a holiday let.

ANECDOTE: After investigating the need for his own website and discovering the large costs involved, John found it was more viable to be listed on an online reservation platform, as this meant he didn't need his own website after all!

CHAPTER 2

Issues to Consider Before Taking the Plunge

The following pages discuss the things you need to consider prior to entering into the holiday-let or B&B market.

....

WHY THE B&B/HOLIDAY-LET INDUSTRY IS BECOMING SO POPULAR

Recent research indicates that people who travel a lot now prefer to stay in a holiday let or B&B when having a short-break holiday. One of the reasons is that they want to understand better the culture of the area they are visiting and, to that end, they expect the property's host to be representative of the local community.

Another reason for the popularity of this industry is that the level of hospitality and facilities offered is often far greater than that provided in most other forms of accommodation.

DECIDING ON THE LOCATION

The vast majority of your guests don't want to drive for more than three hours to reach their destination. Location, therefore, is important when looking to establish your holiday let or B&B outside of a metropolitan city.

Many people prefer staying in city areas, and over the years a significant number of hosts who have holiday lets are targeting the corporate market midweek and the leisure market during the weekends.

A diverse range of people is entering this industry, with more and more professionals deciding that this is a lifestyle choice for them. With the rise of online reservation platforms, an increasing number of people are entering this form of accommodation industry without any prior experience. One reason for this trend is that many people are now working from their hi-tech office at home. They decide that their property is well located, and they have a couple of spare bedrooms that, with bathrooms added to them, could serve as holiday-let/B&B accommodation. Or they have a vacant 'grannie' flat at the bottom of the garden, which again would be ideal as a holiday let.

COMPUTER LITERACY

To be effective in business you need to be computer literate, for most of your bookings will come to you via the Internet. Accountancy programs are also important in enabling you to manage your affairs in an orderly manner. They are an essential tool when dealing with your accountant. You may find you need to complete a computer literacy course or to purchase the relevant programs to operate the financial side of your business. For any business, computers are great tracking tools.

EQUAL COMMITMENT

If there are two of you entering this business, then equal commitment is a must; otherwise friction will occur and any tension will be felt by your guests. If it was your holiday, would you want to walk into someone else's war zone?

Having the ability to earn extra income from home is a positive. However, your success depends on two things: your motivation for entering the business to begin with, and whether you are properly prepared to do so.

Not only does your goal need to be uppermost in your mind when opening your holiday let or Bed and Breakfast; you must also have the discipline to separate work from your private life – particularly when your business is in your home.

As you are thinking about becoming an accommodation provider, financial goals are important, just as they are for any successful small business owner. Set clear and attainable goals. At first you will need to complete a feasibility study, setting achievable goals; otherwise you are setting yourself up for disappointment. Your feasibility study, even for a casual enterprise, needs to set out the financial goals clearly for your business, with strategies to help you reach them. A feasibility study is research-based and tests the viability of your business proposition, while a business plan is developed once you have a firm business. A business plan assumes that your feasibility study stacks up.

If this is to be a full-time enterprise, consider both the advantages and disadvantages of being your own boss. There is no doubt that it will place some stresses on your lifestyle in the first few months while you establish a pattern.

Have realistic plans – don't assume that holidaymakers are just waiting for you to open your doors and that you will then be booked up for months ahead. Holiday-let/B&B bookings, for the most part, are built on word-of-mouth and online recommendations, which take time to gather momentum. Until you build a clientele, you need to have a plan as to how you will survive financially. Think about these issues and try to put together a *contingency plan* allowing for a slow flow of guests at first. This may mean that someone in the household needs to continue working.

Having strong communication skills is a must. A host also requires the attributes of a balanced personality. You need to be naturally pleasant and agreeable. If you are the moody type then this way of life may not be to your liking. Conversation needs to avoid political or religious topics. You need to be patient and tolerant and know the difference between making conversation and becoming a nuisance. An invaluable skill to develop is knowing when to close a conversation politely.

ANECDOTE: Julie found when going into the business of a holiday let that staying in a B&B and holiday let herself was valuable. Until then she had not been aware of the importance of the issues the host has to cope with; such things as people arriving at any time of the day or night regardless of the time of arrival having been arranged previously, dealing with fussy guests at breakfast and trouble-shooting noise issues. Staying in such properties herself helped her develop a strategy to deal with these issues; one that could be applied to dealing with other issues as they arose.

As already mentioned, a successful holiday let/B&B is dependent on equal commitment from all those involved in the hosting. If the accommodation is on your property, living on the premises can be distracting enough for an individual, but for those of you with a family, this disruption can be tenfold. One can both run a successful holiday let/B&B and raise a family on the same premises, but it requires family co-operation and understanding.

Have a defined letting period; for example, you might only have guests three nights a week or for forty weeks a year, taking your break in the low season. This limitation will, however, affect your income projections, so you must factor this into your feasibility study and business plan.

Having a separate annexe for your family away from the guest area is an important option to consider if you want to retain family unity. Children should be taught to be polite and friendly to guests at all times, and not to impose on them unless asked. Many couples are escaping children – they won't really want to spend time with yours.

Consider also having a friend or member of the family who can be available to step in and act as a paid caretaker of your holiday let/B&B should you need to get away, or if you are unwell. If you need to hire an experienced casual to mind your operation while you are away, there are a number of professionals who specialise in this.

More and more holiday lets/B&Bs are being run by single people. In some ways you may find working alone easier than working with a family or an uncommitted partner.

> 'Strive not to be a success, but rather to be of value.'
> Albert Einstein

CHAPTER 3

Defining Your Target Market

Before you decide where you buy, what you are going to buy, or what renovations might be required to convert your existing property, you must know if the market, or customer base, can support your effort.

....

CHOOSING THE TYPE OF GUEST YOU WANT TO ATTRACT

What type of guests would you like to attract to your property? The choice is yours – you should at this early stage make this decision. Would you prefer to be servicing the top end of the market or the general holidaymaker? Would you feel more comfortable with corporate clients or with family groups or groups of friends? Your choice of target market will be a vital factor in influencing your decision on where to locate and how to design your premises.

At this point, once you've made your decision as to what type of holiday-let/B&B business you want to run, I suggest a visit to your local tourist information centre to get the most recent tourist data on the visitors your preferred area attracts per year. In doing so, you will find out how long they stay, and what and why they are visiting. The centre should also be able to advise you on how many other holiday lets/B&Bs there are in your area and their average occupancy rate.

At a recent Airbnb conference staged in France, where an estimated five thousand people attended, one factor seemed to stand out: namely, that many tourists want to experience living like the locals.

This can also apply to business travellers. If you want to attract *business* or *corporate clients* you will need to look at your local community and its market potential.

Have you thought about academics? Does your town have a *university* or a *tertiary college*? Introduce yourself to the person responsible for booking the accommodation for these visitors, send them your promotional literature and *invite them to come and stay for a night*. If they enjoy their stay they are more likely to book with you.

If you see your market to be *overseas guests*, then investigate why tourists are attracted to your area. Is it the local markets? Historic areas? Once again, you can determine this by visiting your tourist centre.

Also, find out the average age of the people visiting your area. This information could help you determine the facilities you need to provide if you are to attract this demographic.

Within the tourist sector you may want to specialise in a particular type of tourist, usually a person who is attracted specifically to your area, or who *shares your interest or passion*. Some examples of this are hikers, birdwatchers, history buffs, people wanting a romantic getaway, the gay community.

To target a particular niche you may need to consider the following:

★ Whether you have particular knowledge of that market yourself.
★ Whether you may need to supply special facilities.

If your niche is going to be birdwatching, you may want to consider attractive photos in your hallway of local birds, or maps that show locations of different species and when they gather. A word of caution here. Don't go overboard, as you don't want to put other guests off. A few details here and there will provide a conversation point.

If you choose to promote your property you could launch it into the market through advertising and editorial in appropriate journals. Offer influential people and decision makers within your niche community a weekend away at your establishment. Being listed on the major online reservation platforms is a must, for they generate a lot of bookings.

THE CORPORATE MARKET

Some B&B/holiday-let operators capture the corporate midweek market by canvassing as many businesses in their immediate area that have commercial travellers regularly visiting them. Commercial travellers often look for more 'homely' accommodation in which they feel they are able to relax. A host could consider targeting interest groups within the corporate sector or base their target market on a similar age group to their own. Another option would be to appeal to a sector of the workforce similar to that in which they have been involved themselves.

SINGLE TRAVELLERS

Many single people only experience meaningful company at work; they go home by themselves, to themselves. They need a holiday too, even if it is just to meet and talk to others. You may need to be centrally located and close to transport to attract these guests. Such visitors will usually expect you to provide them with local information about tourist spots and pubs and clubs where they can meet people.

WOMEN TRAVELLERS

The single female traveller offers an ever-growing market – in terms of both their work and leisure activities. Some women, however, feel uncomfortable sitting by themselves having dinner. If they go to a restaurant alone they are in danger of attracting unwanted attention from the opposite sex, but they feel trapped in their room if they order room service. Holiday lets/B&Bs are a great antidote to this, particularly those that offer the option of an evening meal or self-catering facilities.

THE GAY MARKET

The gay market, like any other, can be a lucrative one. It has been a particularly successful target market in the past through advertisements placed in publications appealing to the gay community. Word of mouth works very strongly in this holiday sector.

There are many holiday lets/B&Bs run successfully by gay couples. No proprietor – gay or straight – is allowed to discriminate against gay people, recent legislation having enshrined this in law.

PEOPLE WITH A DISABILITY

Disabled people, like anyone else, enjoy travelling for pleasure or often need to travel for work. Again, this can be a very loyal group, with great word-of-mouth potential. You will need to give careful consideration to the facilities you provide if you wish to cater for this market.

THE FAMILY MARKET

Holiday lets/B&Bs that cater specifically for the family market will usually have well-designed suites that can also revert to separate accommodation. The biggest opportunities are for those who are located in an area where there is a lot for children to do: offering swimming, fishing, horse-riding, bush walking and so forth or close to a major attraction.

Self-contained cottages, where the host might provide a breakfast basket meal, are becoming a very popular choice for families and couples alike.

Farmstay is another popular option to consider – a place to cater for families on a farm. If you go down this road, you could create a storybook farm on your property, with sheep, cats, dogs, pigs and chickens that children can feed, ponies they can ride, and a cow or a goat the children can hand-milk. Appropriate adult supervision for all this is a must.

NO SMOKING

It is advisable to have a non-smoking policy inside the dwelling, with an ashtray in an outside area. Ideally, apply this no-smoking policy to the entire property, inside and out; this is routine in many countries (e.g. the UK, USA, Canada, New Zealand, Australia) and with numerous local authorities.

NO CHILDREN

If you don't wish children to stay, it is best to say, 'We don't have the facilities to cater for children.' If you do want to welcome children, this could be developed as an interesting and lucrative niche market. But remember, children will behave like children and you need to be prepared for what that may mean.

NO PETS

If you have your own pets you will need to advertise this to potential guests. There may be valid reasons why guests prefer to stay where there are no pets. For example, they may be allergic to them. Have handy the name of a local kennel or cattery that houses cats and dogs, so that you can recommend them to potential guests.

Some holiday lets/B&Bs, however, are successfully targeting this market and acting as hosts for animals. This particular market has huge growth potential.

You should advise your insurers that you are catering for animals, as it may have an effect on your annual premium.

ANECDOTE: There are stories of guests being left to their own devices, never sighting the host and therefore finding it difficult to access local knowledge. If you are not going to be in contact with your guests, make sure you collect information on your area, brochures, books, travel timetables and the like, and keep them for guest use. Guests will appreciate information on great walks and local attractions, and having access to books on the history of your area. Some guests will not have a car and will be relying on public transport. Comprehensive information here will be appreciated.

Dare to be different!

CHAPTER 4

Choosing and Preparing Your Property

The first decision you need to make when entering the short-break holiday market is how many rooms you will have to let. This decision will impact on whether you use your existing property or look around for a new one.

USING YOUR CURRENT PROPERTY

The main reason people choose the holiday-let/B&B option is that the house they currently own has sufficient space to accommodate both themselves and potential guests. There are benefits in such an arrangement: your guests have easy access to you, it is easier to keep an eye on your property, and it is not as far to go to work. The negatives are that family life can be impinged on by your guests, and that it can be hard ever to escape from work. Ideally, you need to have private living space for you and your family away from the guest areas.

What is the best option? The main thing you need to consider is privacy. No matter which route you choose – or, due to property or financial constraints, have had chosen for you – you need to ensure you and your family have some personal space where guests are unable to intrude. Your family area would include a bathroom, bedrooms and preferably a separate lounge or family room. Without this space the strain on your personal relationships may be too much to bear. It is also good for your guests, as they are less likely to feel they are intruding on your life. This space is particularly important if you have children or grandchildren living with you.

Self-contained accommodation is becoming more popular with guests due to the separation between guests and hosts.

ARE YOU IN THE RIGHT LOCATION?

You basically have three options to consider, in terms of location, when looking to run a holiday let/B&B:

1 A busy tourist area. If this is your favoured option then be sure to factor into your profit/loss spreadsheet the seasonality factors of people visiting the area.

2 A country town. This option is becoming very popular, as many people have sold their metro-city property at the top of the market cycle and moved into a country town, buying the house of their choice, and still having money left over. They can work from their hi-tech office at home and only need to go to the workplace twice a month or so. Ideally, the town should be within a three-hour drive from a major city.

3 A city suburb. This option has become very popular in recent years, as many people have suitable properties that can be converted for the holiday market. A word of caution: if your property is outside of a ten-mile/sixteen-kilometre distance from the city centre then be sure you are located in a suburb that, for various reasons, attracts visitors; example, beaches, history, light industrial or conferences areas.

ASSESSING YOUR PROPERTY FOR HOLIDAY-LET POTENTIAL

No matter which of the three location options you prefer, you still need to test the viability of getting the property ready for use as a holiday let or a Bed and Breakfast.

First, you need to walk through the dwelling with a pad and pencil, taking notes as you go and looking at internal aspects such as walls, floors, furnishings, general facilities and so forth through the eyes of a paying guest – not you as the owner, for if you do that you will most likely deceive yourself.

For your property to be a roaring success, with good occupancy, you need to appeal to both local and international markets. Ask yourself the following questions about your property, or about the one you are thinking of purchasing:

★ Is the property near a main road or in a country town with easy access?
★ Is the property in a tourist area?

You also need to factor into your profit and loss projections the seasonality of the area.

DECIDING WHETHER TO CONVERT YOUR CURRENT PROPERTY OR BUY OR BUILD A NEW ONE

You need to establish whether you are going to convert or adjust the home you already live in, buy a new place, or custom build a property if you can find suitable land in a suitable location.

Each option has its merits – what you choose will depend on your personal circumstances. If you only want your holiday let/B&B to give you pocket money or be a supplement to an already healthy financial position, it is probably best to convert the property you already have. If you want your property to provide you with a little more financially, and if your house is not in a major city or a tourist area, you may need to consider either buying an existing property or custom building one.

BUYING AN ESTABLISHED HOLIDAY LET/B&B

You have done the research and realised that your home or cottage at the bottom of the garden just won't adequately convert to a holiday let/B&B. Plus you have decided that you want to make this your sole livelihood. You have a bit of money in the bank and you believe the best thing to do is buy an established enterprise. That way you should have a good income from day one.

Ask yourself what percentage of the holiday-let/B&B business is made up of return customers? How much, therefore, are you paying for 'goodwill'; that is, the intangible contribution of the current owners? Is it valid?

- ★ Do the books look accurate? Do the assets outweigh the liabilities? Get the opinion of your solicitor, bank manager, accountant or financial advisor.
- ★ Have all renovations been undertaken with council approval?
- ★ As with the purchase of any property, location is an important thing to consider. You cannot be in an area where the reasons to stay are too limited for the business to be viable. Does the property have the right qualities?
- ★ Is the current operator intimately connected to the success of the holiday let/B&B? Are they surfers who know the best breaks, or history buffs who belong to the local re-enactment society?

ANECDOTE: I was contacted a few years ago by a prospective buyer of a four-guest-room B&B sitting on three acres of land. The asking price was 1.3 million dollars. The buyer wanted to know if I could help them with the purchase, which I agreed to do only if they could let me know how much the vendors wanted for the property and how much for the business.

The buyer informed me that the asking price included the value of the business. I again advised the buyer to find out how much was being asked for the business and how much for the dwelling as separate entities, otherwise they would never know much they paid for either the property or the business. The buyer after several days told me that the vendors wanted 1.1 million dollars for the property and 200,000 dollars for the business. I then advised the buyer to ask around the area to find out whether the amount asked for the property was reasonable and to come back to me with the findings.

It turned out that the asking price was estimated to be 20,000 dollars too much. I then advised the buyer to find out what was included in the asking price of the business – for example, the value of the chattels, past, current and future record of bookings and the past three years of tax returns. It turned out that for the last ten years the vendor had only declared 60 per cent of the income. This purchase ended up with the buyer paying the full amount asked for the property and 32,000 dollars for the business, a significant saving.

IDENTIFYING YOUR PROPERTY

It's imperative to ensure that the name and street number of your establishment is clear to read day or night. Lighting on LARGE house numbers should be a given. Nothing puts guests in a worse mood than being unable to find your establishment if your street name or house number is hidden behind a hedge or cannot be read on a dark, wet night. Illuminated signs and an identifying feature will make your place stand out: e.g. a fishing lodge could have a large illuminated fish at the front gate and two others 500 metres from the approach to the property. There would be no mistaking the place a guest was heading for!

ANECDOTE: All's well that ends well! It was related to me that a couple arrived at their B&B on a dark night at 10 pm after a long journey, only to find no one at home. There appeared to be no entry to the house. Fortunately a neighbour had lights on and was happy to contact the B&B owner and was thus able to help the stranded guests. After a phone call it was discovered that the keys were under the door mat all the time. Although the problem was solved, a negative tone was set for the rest of the stay.

MAKING A GOOD FIRST IMPRESSION

The first glance your guests have of your holiday let/B&B will be the *impression* they will take with them. It won't matter what they find on the inside of your establishment, that first look of your unkempt gardens and a dilapidated fence will stay with them throughout their whole stay. That is if they bother to come in at all. The truth is, first impressions count. What you can get away with in your own home you cannot get away with as a proprietor of any type of accommodation. The outside appearance of your establishment helps to set the tone of your business.

Use the following *checklist* to help ensure that your guests' first impressions are good:

★ Your lawn is mown regularly, the path to your front door is free from overgrown bushes and hedges, and free from cracks and weeds. If your house is made of bricks, be sure they are clean. Repaint when necessary. When you do repaint, don't paint over a problem. It will recur. Cure the problem first, then paint.

★ Your fence is in good condition. Your entrance is free from cobwebs. Letterboxes, door handles and windows are clean and polished.

★ Light bulbs are changed as soon as needed. The outside is well lit at night.

★ The garden is regularly attended, with no dead plants.

★ Any steps or tiling are swept and cleaned regularly – and checked for slipperiness.

★ Signage to car parking and reception is clearly visible.

Your *garden* needs to be as attractive as you can make it. When planning a garden, think about the time you can realistically afford to spend maintaining it, and design it accordingly.

For summer months, it is a good idea to have some garden furniture so that your guests can enjoy the sunshine and have some outdoor privacy. When you don't have any guests, however, there may be times when you and your family can enjoy these outdoor areas together.

> ANECDOTE: A B&B owner I once stayed with in Ireland said the most important thing about your B&B is to have a spotlessly clean front-door step. People always glance down at the step and gaze around the front door, and spotlessness here gives an impression of care and attention to detail.

YOUR ENTRANCE

Your entrance is the first thing your guests will see on arrival at your establishment. It is your chance to impress them from the word go. You want touches that will exude warmth and friendliness. Go for a bunch of fresh flowers, or an original piece of artwork. Source paintings or sculptures from local artists and have an informative leaflet to give away.

Have artworks on display that can be bought, and consider charging a commission for these.

If your hall is narrow it might be a good idea to add a large mirror to help convey a sense of spaciousness. It is important not to go overboard with furniture in an entrance, as it can create an obstacle course when carrying luggage. An umbrella stand and a coat rack or cupboard are ideal additions. Guests will be pleased with your thoughtfulness.

Flooring deserves special consideration in your porch and hallway. You want a surface that is easy to keep clean and is hard wearing. Tiles need to be non-slip; if you have floorboards you must ensure any polish is not slippery. If you choose carpet you should investigate commercial carpet; it is more durable and easier to keep clean than domestic-grade carpets.

Heating or cooling is another consideration. If you are surrounded by snow you want your entry to feel like a warm cocoon. Likewise, if it happens to be hot and humid you want your guests' first impression to be one of coolness and freshness.

If your entry is a public one serving an apartment block, the same principles apply.

ANECDOTE: When guests arrived at a well-known holiday let, their names were on a small blackboard, near the bell at the front door. There was also a warm message of welcome. This immediately made them feel they were going to have a lovely stay!

LIVING ROOMS

In traditional B&Bs if at all possible, for both your sanity and that of your guests, provide some separate space, other than bedrooms, for the guests to relax in. I would suggest that the best option would be a *lounge* room, or seating area in the breakfast room. For some properties, it might be your old family room, conservatory or former children's playroom. This room will give your guests space and allow them to feel more at home. The fact that this means you will also retain a separate lounge room gives you a place to escape that feels all yours, not the property of the general public.

If it is not practical to have a separate room, the guestroom would ideally be large enough to have a couple of comfortable chairs. This will make it feel more of a sanctuary, and will prevent guests from feeling trapped in a small space.

Research indicates that most guests don't mind sharing living-room areas with each other, providing they can identify where they can sit. For example, if you have a living area available for two guest bedrooms, then rearrange your furniture so that you have two settings. Guests generally don't mind if other guests share their space, or even if it is possible to overhear their conversation.

You could consider providing *entertainment facilities*, particularly music. An assortment of books is a great idea, covering all genres. Board games and cards are a good idea, especially for guests who choose not to go out at night. *Television* is another thing you will need to consider. Many people go to holiday lets/B&Bs to escape from television, but others find it relaxing. My suggestion would be that if you are going to have televisions, place them in the guest bedrooms (preferably in a cupboard) where guests can make the choice to use them, or have a separate TV room. If, because of space limitations, you have to put a TV in the lounge room, don't arrange all your seating to face it.

One of my concerns is that of 'amenity creep'. Some B&Bs are emulating the atmosphere found in motels/hotels from the lower end of the market. Don't do this, because people who choose to stay in small, homely accommodation do so for the home comforts and to avoid the impersonal atmosphere of a hotel. For example, avoid a TV in a guest bedroom that swivels out from the wall. Although it is in fashion to hang a TV set on the wall, many people do not like this. The height is often not correct for viewing.

People love to sit around an *open fire*, so if you have one, be sure to light it, particularly on dull or cold days. This would be a memorable feature of your lounge room and a source of good publicity for you. If you have it, flaunt it!

Likewise, if you have a view of the ocean or mountains, exploit it! Such things are what guests go away for – the romantic ideal of home.

DINING ROOMS

As the name suggests, a vitally important part of a traditional B&B is one meal: breakfast. This meal needs to be taken in a place that characterises the ambience of your establishment. As much care should be taken with the dining facility, be it a dining room or an eat-in kitchen, as with the breakfast itself.

In Airbnb-listed properties the makings of breakfast are often left on the counter or in a designated place in the refrigerator for the guest to help themselves.

A welcoming ambience is very important for dinner, if you are planning to offer this as an option. People will occasionally bring their own wine and, over a few glasses, feel happy talking with strangers.

When buying furniture, be aware of the upkeep. If your table is wood it will require work – you will need to protect it from moisture and heat. When looking to replace furniture, you should consider new furnishings that meet higher fire-resistance standards; ask your local fire authority if in doubt.

You can get some great buys at places such as second-hand shops. You also have the option of buying from a manufacturer or supplier of commercial catering furniture.

For chairs, particularly, this may provide the best option for a larger establishment, as they will be comfortable, practical and hardwearing.

Ensure your dining room has a *sideboard* or bench of some kind. It makes it much easier when clearing tables and serving meals. It also has the added advantage of holding your dinner sets and cutlery. The only word of caution would be not to clutter the top with too many decorative items – keep it simple. If you have too much on it, guests will find it difficult actually to use it.

The *crockery* you use can demonstrate to your guests the style of your establishment. Remember, it is the small things that your guests will describe to their friends. We would suggest crockery is of commercial quality. Any patterns should be under a thick glaze and able to withstand dishwashers at high temperatures. Tapered edges are more prone to chipping, so if you or your partner are clumsy, we would suggest choosing crockery with a rolled edge. Enquire in a retail outlet if there is a piece of china that could be tested for durability. The glazing can be assessed by running a knife across a glazed surface and seeing if it marks.

Do not scrimp on china by buying the cheapest, and, whatever you do, don't buy end-of-line china. Pieces will chip and break; you also need a set for which you can easily purchase replacements or additions as required. Remember you want china that is oven-proof, particularly if you are planning to offer dinner, and any china with a metal embossing, such as a gold rim, may not be suitable to put in a microwave or dishwasher.

Buy some beautiful serving plates and dishes. Using beautiful cutlery and glasses and the best table linen will set the tone for your property – choose a style of china, glassware and linen that reflects the style of your home and that, perhaps, is distinctive of your region. Many period homes are B&Bs; using china, glassware and linen in these that is in keeping with the period of the home will enhance the pleasure of the guests' stay.

Your *glasses* should complement your china. In some cases, where a holiday let/B&B does not have an alcohol licence, guests may be able to bring alcohol, with your permission, whether you provide an evening meal or not. At the very least, you will need glasses for a variety of drinks.

Cutlery needs special consideration. Again, I would suggest easy care. Stainless steel is much easier to look after than silver, not least because you will be able to put it in the dishwasher. It will still stain and smear, however. To minimise this, a good tip is to use boiling hot water and vinegar and wipe it with a linen tea towel once a week after it has been cleaned in a dishwasher. Ornate designs can look wonderful, but are more difficult to keep clean. Choose cutlery made in one piece, as grease and bacteria have a tendency to get caught between the blade and the handle. Plastic, bone and wooden handles are not always a good idea, as they will not withstand the dishwasher. As you can see, you need to balance style considerations with practical ones. Do you want to be cleaning that beautiful silver cutlery every day? Remember that you do want the table to look special when set, so choose wisely.

THE KITCHEN

While design and size of *kitchen* will vary tremendously in small holiday accommodations, this is still a major cog in the machine. Your kitchen may be used for cooking only or may have an eat-in function, or in the case of self-catering and Airbnb will be used by the guest. If you have a family, an eat-in kitchen may not be suitable for both the family and their guests for privacy reasons.

The main thing you need to ensure is *cleanliness*. If you are providing food for the general public, you need to treat this with the seriousness it deserves. The last thing you want is to risk food poisoning. Find out your local authority's regulations to see what restrictions will affect you in your kitchen. With governing bodies looking at the registering of small accommodation providers, increasingly there is a legal require-ment for those preparing or providing food for the general public to obtain a recognised qualification. This will cover all aspects of food handling, storage and preparation. The larger your establishment, the more likely you will be affected by commercial laws of some kind or another.

When catering for a number of guests the minimum requirement is a dishwasher, a microwave and an extractor fan. You might also need to consider a bigger fridge, and a pantry. Your kitchen will need to include a large bench and/or table, as you will need significant workspace.

Safety in any area of life is a key consideration. Kitchens need to be safe places for you, your staff and your guests to work. Kitchens and bathrooms are the most dangerous places in a home. Flooring needs special attention; for example, any tiles need to be of the non-slip vari-ety. Make sure that all of your electrical equipment is safe.

Some authorities currently require your average residential B&B to install a double sink and a dishwasher. High-quality detergent must be used due to the fact that the average dishwasher bought for the home does not heat to 77 degrees Celsius. Properties that offer an evening meal require all the above, but the dishwasher might need to be semi-industrial, depending on the number of rooms you let. These regulations currently do not apply to holiday lets, Airbnb or other reservation sites.

Properties that have a restaurant will need to comply with standard restaurant regulations.

BATHROOMS AND TOILETS

The days of expecting your guests to share the family *bathroom* are numbered. That is not to say you can't be a holiday let/B&B if you don't have separate bathrooms or en-suites for each guestroom. It means that you may not be able to have a room rate that is viable or an occupancy rate that is acceptable. In my experience, many Airbnb properties operate with a bathroom shared between the family and the guest. The room rate in these properties is usually lower and the occupancy rate may not be very high.

If you do elect to run with the family bathroom proposition then be sure you have sufficient cabinets that hide the family's gear. If it's a grand and elegant property you have in mind, and the room rate reflects this, then the guest's expectation will be to access a fully equipped bathroom. This may include a spa bath.

For those who are investigating holiday let/B&B as a long-term option, to misquote Shakespeare, 'to en-suite or not to en-suite, that is the question'! If you can only afford to do one major thing to convert your family home into this form of accommodation, installing en-suites is what you should spend your money on. More bookings are lost for not having en-suites than for any other reason, especially with international travellers. Guests will happily pay more for this option.

If you intend to accommodate people with disabilities, the bathroom and toilet facilities will need special consideration. You will need to consider safety rails, a hand-held showerhead and widened doorways. Floor tiles need to be non-slip and to have no steps, to allow for wheelchair access and ramps up to the doorway.

Given that you will have heating in your bathroom, you will also need an extractor fan to eradicate all the condensation that occurs. Opening a window is not sufficient to maintain the controlled ventilation required to keep condensation and, in the long-term, mould at bay in bathrooms. If you have sufficient room between your bathroom ceiling and the roof, the most efficient way to cover heating, ventilation and lighting is by installing a three-in-one heater, fan and light. For a little extra expenditure you will have a bathroom that is well lit, warm and well ventilated.

We would suggest that you replace shower curtains with doors, as there is less chance for errant water, and thus accidents, to occur. Also, avoid showers over your bath. These can be another safety nightmare and prove difficult for some people to manage. If you must use shower curtains, ensure that you wash them regularly. Nothing puts a guest off more than mould. Also, ensure that shower curtains are weighted at the bottom, so as not to wrap around your guests' legs when they are having a shower.

It is important to have efficient, easy-to-operate showers. Taps with a simple single action are the best ones. The flow of water from the showerhead also needs to be adequate. It is very hard to rinse long hair with a trickle of water! You need to ensure you have a copious supply of hot water. Water temperature needs to be checked; water that is too hot can lead to scalds. This is not an area where one can economise. And guests will always remember the holiday where they had a cold shower.

ANECDOTE: Continental showers are more varied and complicated to operate than those in the Antipodes. For southern international travellers especially, make sure they know how to operate the shower. There have been several stories of guests reduced to a flannel wash during their stay as they could not negotiate the showers' taps! And we all know how Australian guests, in particular, love to shower!

All your doors should be fitted with locks, and windows should be made of opaque glass or fitted with blinds. The locks are particularly important if guests are sharing a bathroom.

You may also need to consider adding power points to large bathrooms. Special waterproof points are available and can be a legal requirement. At the very least, you need sufficient power points for two appliances: a shaver and a hairdryer.

Ideally, the bathroom area should be self-contained. This gives a classier atmosphere to the room than the situation in Europe where you often find the hand basin in the bedroom.

When it comes to furniture in your bathroom, it should be kept to a minimum. However, you might like to consider a chair or a stool. Ensure they won't be affected adversely by the dampness.

With bathrooms and en-suites it is the extras that will win you brownie points with your guests. We suggest that you consider providing the following:

★ Two good-quality, generously sized towels per person, which you change regularly. You also need to provide a hand towel and face cloths.
★ Mini soaps and hair products, preferably from a place like a body shop or another aromatherapy retailer. You might even be lucky enough to find a local person who makes natural products. These will need to be changed after each guest. The provision of soap and hair product dispensers is a good alternative. So far these have been sadly lacking in most Airbnb properties I have experienced.
★ Make-up remover pads. This is a great idea, as it will prevent your guests using your towels for this purpose.
★ Plenty of thick, luxurious-feeling toilet paper. OK, so it's a hidden luxury. All too many accommodation providers get this wrong. Don't scrimp and buy the cheap brand. Your guests will notice and will not be impressed. Ensure your spare rolls are in an easy-to-find place.

Fresh flowers, preferably from your garden, or a small plant, will brighten up the room and reinforce the impression that you are the nurturing type. Be aware that some guests may be allergic to fresh flowers, so you may want to advise them beforehand.

BEDROOMS

If you are going after the luxury romantic-getaway market you might consider having spa baths for each guest bedroom. At the high end of the market, they are a definite draw card. You can, of course, get a higher room rate for the privilege.

In many countries, approved B&Bs have a minimum bedroom size and spaciousness requirements that are as follows:

★ Single rooms: 5.6 square metres/60 square feet
★ Double rooms: 8.4 square metres/90 square feet
★ Twin rooms: 10.2 square metres/110 square feet

So far, these requirements are not impacting on the Airbnb market.

Now to the 'bed' part of your property, the place where your guests will spend at least one-third of their stay with you. The bed is the most important investment in furniture you will make in any area of the accommodation industry – and you really must consider buying new ones. It is your guests' opinion of the quality of your bed that you will most be recommended for, or otherwise.

> ANECDOTE: It's very important to have rooms set apart specifically for your holiday let. Jenny was not thrilled when in conversation with the host she realised she was sleeping in the host's bed!

One of the most common questions I get asked is: what should you look for when purchasing a bed? First, buy wholesale – you will get a better price and a more durable mattress.

It is worth noting, especially for those running a B&B, that as soon as you register your business you will gain allowances with a wide range of wholesalers, from bed linen and bed manufacturers, to hospitality suppliers. Take advantage of these and shop around.

I suggest you buy contract quality. These beds have the added advantage of being built for multiple and varied sleepers – so they will last you longer in the long run. Most importantly, they are reinforced around the sides – the first place your guests will sit when entering their guestroom.

If you have a number of guestrooms, purchase queen beds – doubles are too small for most couples – and have at least one room with two single beds that will zip up into a queen- or king-size bed. With more and more friends travelling together, along with mothers and daughters and sons, the ability to offer twin beds will give your potential guests another reason to stay with you. The single zip-up model has the option of an all-over covering. All commercial beds should be Health Shield protected, which protects against the build-up of mould, mildew, bacteria and dust mites. Commercial bed coverings are fire retardant.

A rack or suitable place for luggage in the guest bedroom is important. This prevents suitcases ending up on the bed, bringing with them dust or dirt from outside.

You will need to supply electric blankets during the colder months. You need two pillows per person. You need at least two sets of bed linen per bed – more if you don't want to wash every day.

Think seriously about domestic linen if you are a larger establishment. It will need to withstand the daily washes, and coloureds will fade very quickly. Remember, white linen can always be bleached.

Normal household bed sheets have an average life expectancy of 300 washes, while those used in the hospitality industry are expected to last for over 400 washes – they tend to be 50 per cent polyester and 50 per cent cotton. There are a number of linen suppliers to the hospitality industry. Look them up in the telephone directory or online. Ensure that you have spares of everything (blankets, pillows, sheets) in a cupboard in the guestroom in case the guest's preference is for something different from the bedding provided.

It is important to have a sheet and a light blanket as an alternative to a continental quilt. Many guests find even light quilts too hot.

Floors should be carpeted or have rugs to help absorb noise and keep the room warmer in winter. It is very important that your window coverings, whether they are curtains or blinds, give total darkness in daylight. Your guests will probably want to sleep in and you need to ensure they can do so with ease.

You need bedside lights that are suitable for use as reading lamps on both sides of the bed, and plenty of accessible power points to cater for everything people travel with. I have stayed in many holiday lets and B&Bs over the years where it was impossible to read by the lamp provided. Don't hide power points under the bed or behind furniture! What you don't want is double adaptors – they are extremely dangerous. If you need multiple points, use a power board, as they usually have a power-surge switch. All guest bedrooms should have a source of heating and cooling, with clear directions if needed.

If possible, guest bedrooms should have locks on their doors. If your guests are staying for more than one night they will want to keep personal effects in their room. They may feel they can't if there is no lock on the door, and other people can access their space.

As for general furniture, an absolute requirement is a wardrobe, as most guests travel with clothing that needs to be hung. A small wardrobe will suffice. You should supply at least five good-quality hangers per guest, definitely not the bent-wire variety!

Bedside tables are important, with a tallboy or shelves for folded items. A chair can be very useful, and a desk is often appreciated – pens and notepaper are a nice addition. Don't forget the wastepaper basket in every room. An adequate mirror is also essential!

When it comes to extras – think of everything you would like in the perfect bedroom and try to provide it. A jug and glasses is always appreciated. Mints are a good idea or a chocolate on the pillow. This simple thoughtfulness often comes up in conversation when B&Bs are mentioned. Tissues are essential.

Mini CD players or iPod docks are also appreciated. If you want to go all out you could provide guest robes, a must when guests have to go out of their room to access the bathroom.

Some people also appreciate facilities to make their own coffee and tea in their room.

HOME OFFICE

It is a good idea to set up a *home office*. You will need a space where you can do your paperwork, set up your computer and any other equipment you might need. The tax system requires you to keep precise records of your business activities and it is a sensible idea to have a dedicated room in which to do this.

Your accountant/financial consultant will be able to advise whether or not there is a tax benefit here; there very likely will be.

How and where you set this up is a personal choice. My suggestion would be that you do not put this equipment in your bedroom. Your holiday let/B&B will invade much of your personal space and you need one room in your house that is dedicated for work so that commercial activities do not invade other areas of your life.

CHAPTER 5

Viability and Local Bodies

DECIDING WHETHER YOUR PROPERTY IS VIABLE

By now you have probably worked out how much the renovations are going to cost, including any tradespeople's charges. After adding it all up, you find that it is totally unaffordable – well, at least you know. If this is the case and you still want to be a small accommodation provider then you need to readjust your expectations or look for a property in the right location that is affordable – remember, it's a straightforward business decision.

If it transpires that it is viable to adjust your property for holiday-let/B&B purposes, ask the tradespeople when they are likely to start and finish their tasks – if they say six weeks, then add another three weeks onto their estimate. You need a firm start date; the finish date can be negotiated, as situations often change due to unforeseen circumstances.

BUILDING AND DEVELOPMENT APPLICATIONS

Authorities are now considering new regulations that may be applied to properties listed with online reservation platforms. Before an authority adopts a code or policy it usually goes through a process of community exposure and consultation. The trouble here is that most would-be proprietors show little interest in these things until their proposed plan is directly affected. It's always better to obtain all the information early in developing your holiday-let/B&B ideas to enable you to adapt your plans and satisfy requirements.

Approval has traditionally been granted to operate a home occupation (run by yourself) or a home industry (where you might employ other people). In granting this approval, authorities would again consider local amenity issues. For example, would it be noisy, have a lot of traffic coming and going, or incur other nuisance or environmental issues? Of course there are some informal, unapproved operations in existence, which authorities might not actively pursue, unless they get a complaint about them.

If it's your intention to renovate or expand your property, read the information below for your guidance.

LOCAL BODIES, HOLIDAY LETS AND B&BS

Most of the online reservation platforms do not require you to seek local government approval, but do recommend that their listed property owners abide by local government rules and regulations, as local bodies are looking at ways to enforce acceptable requirements regarding small accommodation providers. As a host, always remember your obligation regarding your duty of care in law. This means you must be aware of guest safety at all times. For example, ensure that fire safety precautions are met and that food handling and storage comply with local hygiene regulations. Being up to date with local government requirements is in your and your guests' best interests.

Currently, local and state governments are in the process of producing White Papers designed to address the impact that the sharing economy is having on society. For the future, one can expect new rules and regulations that will be enforceable. These will be adjusted from current Bed and Breakfast requirements to include short holiday lets.

In the meantime, abide by the rules and regulations set down by local government when renovating or expanding your dwelling to accommodate guests. There is evidence that governments are seeking to regulate this sector of accommodation in response to the rise of the online reservation platform. Certainly authorities are looking closely at this market as I write, and the situation regarding regulation is changing from one day to the next.

Before you march headlong into deciding where you are going to set up your holiday let/B&B, or whether you are going to convert your current home, you need to check the requirements of your local authority and how these may apply to you.

First, there is a raft of planning permission and building regulations if you are considering structural changes to an existing dwelling or adding an extension; it is vital that you contact your local authority for their advice and/or permission. Another suggestion is to get a copy of the relevant authority's planning approval guide.

APPROVAL AND CONSTRUCTION OF HOLIDAY AND B&B ACCOMMODATION

The most daunting part of becoming a small accommodation provider might be dealing with your local authority. It sounds pretty simple to set aside a couple of bedrooms, advertise in the local paper, and in roll the customers. But don't forget the way the sharing economy is trending. Some authorities already have policies in place to deal with the accommodation side of the sharing economy. In future you will probably need the approval of local authorities before you start operations; otherwise, before you know it, an officer will be knocking on your door and asking for an explanation. At this stage it is better to anticipate future requirements than to find that, down the track, you are not permitted to operate.

Currently you will generally need to obtain *planning approval* for the use of the premises as a B&B, plus building approval if any structural alterations or other modifications to the building are necessary. The good news is that in certain jurisdictions you can make a combined application for both planning and building approval, which should speed up the process. In some instances, the approvals, and certainly the building component, can be obtained through a private certifier. Private Certification is being considered for Airbnb as I write.

A lot of the codes and policies are now written in a performance format, which means that authorities give you a series of objectives and some suggested ways of meeting those objectives. You have the flexibility to decide what you will do to achieve the requirements. However, you may still encounter some prescriptive requirements – which simply state what you must do. While this format removes any doubts about getting it right, it also takes away some of the opportunity for flexibility and innovation.

You will be hard pressed persuading authorities of the merits of your vision for your individual establishment if it deviates in some way from the rules that have been set down. Appeal rights against an authority's decision may vary and become so costly and time-consuming as to make your proposal not viable. It would be much better to negotiate as much as possible in the initial stages.

The thing to be aware of is that different parts of a building can have different classifications depending on their uses. This can have important implications for the final classification of a building and the required type of construction.

FIRE SAFETY

Currently, local government fire safety guides and publications will tell you what you have to do to comply with fire safety law, assistance in carrying out a fire risk assessment and identifying the general fire precautions you need to have in place. In many countries it is a legal requirement to have fire alarms in your home. At the very least, you would be required to install a system of hard-wired *smoke alarms* in every guest bedroom and in hallways associated with guest bedrooms.

If there is no hallway, smoke alarms would need to be installed in areas between guest bedrooms and the remainder of the building, and between each storey. The smoke alarms in hallways and areas outside of guest bedrooms may also be required to incorporate a light to be activated by the smoke alarm; alternatively, the smoke alarms can be wired to activate existing hallway lighting to assist evacuation of the occupants in the event of a fire.

In essence, a building used by the public must strictly adhere to all fire regulations, providing fire extinguishers and smoke alarms, and sometimes it may be required to install fire doors and have designated evacuation points. Bedroom windows in some areas must be designed to act as emergency exits. In large establishments, fire alarms may be connected directly to the local fire station.

Fire blankets should be of a size to meet the expected risk. Your local Fire Brigade, fire authority or specialist fire-fighting supply and installation companies should guide you in your selection and installation of both fire extinguishers and fire blankets.

Currently, it is a requirement of the fire authority – and certainly in your own interests to limit liability – to have fire safety measures inspected by an appropriately qualified person who can certify that such measures are capable of working properly. Depending on the nature, extent and location of any additions or alterations that you might want to carry out on your building, the authority may also require you to upgrade the fire protection between your building, any associated structures on your land and adjoining properties. This will depend on the existing and proposed separation between the buildings and property boundaries.

Of necessity, this information is of a general nature only and may not be directly applicable to individual circumstances, in which case individuals should seek expert advice. Those planning on holiday lets/B&Bs will need to check any new legislation and its application at the time of any proposed development.

ANECDOTE: When looking into the cost of renovating his property, Robert found it resulted in a market price over and above the reasonable value of similar properties in his area. He did some sums and found that, even though this was the case at the time, in the future his profits from his holiday let would make renovations worthwhile.

You must be able to see the potential of the property. Some people are better at this than others, but there are ways to learn. There is no point in listening to someone else convincing you of potential if you can't see it yourself. Ask lots of questions and clarify all points you are not sure of.

Consult a professional before you purchase, or before you make the decision to renovate. Speak to an architect or builder, or even someone you know as a seasoned renovator, to get an understanding of the achievable and possible, and what it will cost to arrive at your dream. Unless you have a sound understanding of housing structure, get a qualified building inspection done, and include this as a condition of purchase.

Balance your renovations between personal requirements and general market appeal. Over-specialising your property will narrow your resale market considerably. Will the furniture that you need to buy to create the finished effect fit into the room? You would be surprised how many people have ordered furniture that will not go through their doorways! On one notable occasion in England, a large lounge suite had to be moved in via the window.

Consider the layout of the house. It is much easier and cheaper to embellish the original layout of the house than to completely reinvent the entire house. Remember that the most expensive part of any renovation is the labour content. The more work you can do yourself, the cheaper your renovation will be.

To be realistic, set yourself a time frame, and then double it. This applies to using contractors, and more so to the 'do-it-yourself' (DIY) renovator. A 'simple' job seldom is, and untold catastrophes can occur. Furthermore, the constraints of full-time work, raising a family and social commitments can see your time allocated for renovating ebb and flow – so too your enthusiasm.

Be careful what building company you use. Always get more than one tradesperson to advise and quote you for the work required.

If the work you are having carried out is on a large scale, you should consult a surveyor. However, if you have just moved into your home, you should already have had a structural survey done.

Take into consideration that some renovations may require planning permission and may have to satisfy building regulations; for example, a new roof covering. The planning department in your locality will be able to advise you.

PLANNING PERMISSION

How much you can extend the dwelling will depend on your local authority and their individual policy. It also depends on the property type you wish to alter. There can be different limits on bungalows; apartments; semi-detached, detached, end-of-terrace and terraced properties.

There is not always a need to gain *planning permission* as some extension work, e.g. loft conversions and small extensions in some countries, can be done under *Permitted Development*. This allows you to build a certain amount without submitting plans. Each government or local authority has a different, and definite, policy on what meterage is acceptable.

If you don't need to get planning permission, then a *'certificate of lawful development'* can be issued to you. It will show that you have submitted plans and that you were legally allowed to carry out the works.

ANECDOTE: A B&B networking group came up with the idea of occasionally spending the night in each other's guestrooms, testing the room's appeal, the condition of the bed and the bathroom facilities. This helped all of them gauge the service they were offering against their respective room rate, and enabled them to bounce ideas off each other for improvements that could be made.

CHAPTER 6

Planning for Success

Over the past few years, speaking to hundreds of prospective holiday-let/B&B owners, I have often faced the dilemma of how to sound enthusiastic about people's prospective ventures, while still issuing a word of caution.

·····················

To many people, owning and operating a small holiday establishment, more than any other venture, represents a romantic ideal. I see normally rational people – doctors, lawyers, business owners, teachers, police officers and process workers – about to take huge financial risks on a venture for which they have not written a feasibility study or business plan.

No matter what your financial or personal expectations for your new venture, it is a business and you need to treat it with the gravity it deserves. This is true for long-term or short-term ventures. You still need to apply the same principles if your holiday accommodation only operates for a short time; for example, the time it takes for you to save up for that overseas holiday. You will find it impossible to achieve the results you want without a blueprint on how you plan to get there.

BEING PREPARED

If there is one piece of advice that I would give you it is: '*BE PREPARED*'. More businesses fail due to lack of planning and ongoing financial management than for any other reason.

So why don't people plan to succeed? The main reason cited is time, or the lack of it. MAKE TIME. This is your life or livelihood we are talking about. A few extra months planning your venture, researching the business you are thinking of entering, WILL make the difference between success and failure.

Get out a notebook and write down your answers to the following questions:

★ Do you have any business experience? Write down how you believe you can use this experience in your business.

★ Do you have any other experiences you can draw on? How do you believe they will help you?

★ Have you spoken to an accountant, financial advisor or business consultant?

★ Have you contacted your region's tourism office to get information on your area's tourism statistics?

★ Have you contacted your local authority to get their position on small accommodation enterprises?

★ Have you spoken to at least five other operators about their holiday-let/B&B experience?

★ Have you stayed in other holiday lets/B&Bs? This is important so that you can test the adequacy of your facilities, especially the bedroom, specifically the bed, and the bathroom, against your perceptions. Write down the things you believe these properties are doing well, and the things you believe they could improve on. Ensure that your plan addresses these issues.

★ Why do you believe there is a demand for another holiday let or B&B in your area? What will be your main advantage over your competitors?

★ Have you spoken to the Bed and Breakfast or Tourist Association in your chosen area? Have you contacted the national office?

★ Is your holiday let/B&B to be a lifestyle change or a commercial venture in the stand-alone sense?

★ Have you determined the financial goals you have for the business?

★ Have you spoken to a range of people who have stayed in a holiday let or a B&B to assess their expectations?

★ Have you spoken to friends and acquaintances who have their holiday lets listed with online reservation platforms to ascertain their experiences?

★ Have you discussed with your financial advisor or business consultant the effect that turning your house into a business will have on your financial affairs?

- ★ Have you worked out how much it will cost you to turn your house into a holiday let/B&B? Did you get three quotes for all work you are not going to do yourself?
- ★ Have you worked out a financial plan to supplement your income while you build your business?

FINANCING YOUR VENTURE

In the first year of your new enterprise you should try and *finance* your venture yourself. However, if additional funding is necessary you need to ensure you contact your small business association or consultant, your bank or building society, or a financial advisor. Remember, all start-up businesses need initial seed capital, and a small accommodation enterprise is no exception.

You need to take the answers to all the questions above to any meetings you have regarding finance. It will demonstrate that you have done your preparation and will keep you focused.

USING YOUR BUSINESS PLAN

This written outline of your business idea is designed to help you focus more clearly on what exactly you are planning in your holiday-let/B&B operation. How would you describe your idea to someone else? Why will your proposal be different from other holiday-let/B&B operations? Why should people want to stay with you? What will you offer them, apart from somewhere to stay? In short, why will your enterprise be successful? Do you have an analysis of your long-term and short-term goals?

YOUR PROFESSIONAL SUPPORT

The success of any business operation can be directly linked to accessing quality professional support. You will need key advisors and mentors to assist you in formulating your ideas, guiding your progress and watching over you, and giving you not only feedback, but, most importantly, someone to talk to. Professionals you may need to consult will include: your accountant or financial advisor; a solicitor; a banker; insurance agent/broker; a B&B Association representative (these associations deal with most forms of small accommodation); a business mentor or paid advisor; and, when you are ready, carefully selected tradespeople for their input.

YOUR ACCOUNTANT

Your *accountant* should be one of your key advisors, as he or she can advise you on: your preferred legal structure (sole trader, partnership, company, trust), your financial and funding options, your approach to a financial source, spreadsheets/books and control systems, taxation requirements, registrations and returns (including VAT/GST – Goods and Services Tax – returns where applicable), capital gains etc. if applicable, financial reporting and forecasts, and superannuation options. We suggest you look around for an accountant to whom you can relate: someone who can speak your language, answer your questions and, most importantly, not too busy to return your calls and give you help and advice *when* you need it.

YOUR SOLICITOR

If you consult a *solicitor*, he/she can be used to check any contract, especially leases, before you sign. We are, whether we like it or not, living in an age of litigation, and the best legal insurance you can arrange is to have a good solicitor. You should also use your solicitor to assist you when you construct your own legal checklist.

You may need to access funds; remember, the banking industry is changing weekly and it is unlikely that you will have access to a bank manager. You will probably be dealing with a lending or a relationship officer, who will be charged with looking after your account. Try and foster a good relationship with your contact person, but before you reach this stage, have a good look around to see which bank is the best for you and your needs.

INSURANCE

As far as *insurance* is concerned, remember that it is a highly competitive market. We suggest that you should look at obtaining at least three quotes before you sign up. We also suggest that you check with your local tourism authority and/or other small accommodation operators to obtain the names of the insurance companies they use and are prepared to recommend.

B&B AND TOURISM AUTHORITIES

It is worth considering your *B&B Association/Tourism Authority* as a source of industry support, networking and the backup you will require if you want to succeed in the industry. Being a member gives access to market research, industry news, training, workshops and best practices by networking with others in the industry.

A GOOD BUSINESS MENTOR

For large-scale holiday lets, having a *good business mentor* or a paid advisor is only now being recognised as one of the keys to business success. A business mentor is simply someone with knowledge and empathy who is available to act as a coach, a guide, a motivator and a sounding board. It is someone who can discuss your business and management ideas with you and help you make informed and effective decisions. This could also work for a listing on a reservation site – e.g. Airbnb – gaining insights into how this particular system operates. Your mentor need not be someone specialising in the accommodation industry. It should, however, be someone with business experience who can pass on advice, opinions and information to help make you a better manager.

CHAPTER 7

Hosting Issues to Consider

PROVIDING INFORMATION FOR YOUR PROPERTY LISTING

Most online reservation platforms make it very easy to list your property, with prompts to help. You will also need to upload some meaningful pictures of your property along with general but salient property information; for example, the provision of meals.

FEATURES AND BENEFITS

You may be asked about alcohol, whether it can be bought nearby, or if it is BYO.

Some guests, especially from abroad, may ask whether there are cooking facilities they can use, a small kitchenette, or BBQ in summer. Any extras you provide such as laundry facilities, irons, hairdryers, phone lines, Internet access, etc., also need to be detailed here. If you have special packages for honeymoons, corporate clients, special school events or particular interests, now is the time to offer to tell your potential guest about them – you can also list these features when you upload the property's pictures onto the reservation platform.

ANECDOTE: A young guest had a very happy stay in New York due to the holiday-let host going to some trouble to point out local bars where friendly locals drank and that also sold good food. The host provided maps of the area and indicated interesting walking routes to local destinations.

CHILDREN, PETS OR SMOKING?

By now you will have determined your policy on these issues, and you need to detail these to all prospective bookings. Better your guests know your stance in advance rather than having a possible confrontation when they arrive.

SPECIAL NEEDS AND REQUIREMENTS

If you don't have appropriate facilities (such as wheelchair access) you need to advise this by how your information is worded. For example, your information could start with: 'We are on the upper floor of . . .' And go on from there.

DIETARY ISSUES

Dietary specialities are another thing you may be asked to cater for. If you provide an evening meal you may wish to ask at the point of reservation whether any of the party have any food restrictions, so you can plan in advance.

LOCAL ACTIVITIES AND ATTRACTIONS

You need to know *everything* about your local area, as guests will expect you to know it well. Many guests do not arrive by car and so rely on public transport. Have information such as taxi and hire-car contacts, and bus and train timetables available.

Sell the best parts of your locality to your potential guests, as this could sway them in your direction, either beforehand or during the duration of their stay. You also need to be able to provide details of great places to eat in your area. Guests may ask you to send menus of local pubs and restaurants or even make bookings for them. Sharing your knowledge of local theatre groups and entertainment venues will be appreciated by your guests.

DEPOSITS AND CANCELLATIONS

The online reservation platforms will expect you to honour bookings made and will contact the pending guest if your circumstances change.

Some booking agencies can have lengthy deposit and cancellation policies; it is imperative you check this.

When dealing with your guests there are a number of things you can do that will help you to achieve the perception of fantastic service. Ideally, when the guests arrive, and after they have freshened up, show them around and suggest that they come and join you for a quality drink and some freshly baked goodies. Offering morning and afternoon tea has multiple purposes: it will allow you to get to know one another; you can find out what your guests intend to do while staying in your area; and it gives you the opportunity to offer suggestions about local attractions.

BEHAVIOUR

This is where your people skills come in. If your guests look like they want to be left alone then respect their privacy. If, on the other hand, your guests want to chat, then remember they'll be doing so in your time; you may need to determine the duration. This is a skill you will need to master.

You need always to work as quietly as possible. When guests come and stay with you, they are there to relax. They will often read, sleep in or just rest. You want to minimise any negative impact you may have on them.

ANECDOTE: Friends of mine once stayed at a holiday let while the owner was renovating. This became a very noisy, dusty and uncomfortable stay. Our friends vowed never to return!

When it comes to conversation there are a few golden rules:

★ Never talk about religion, sex or politics until it is safely established that these topics are acceptable. Don't be baited into getting into these topics with your guests. Such discussions usually end badly.
★ Be friendly and nice, but don't over-host; present an aura of friendliness that doesn't tip over into familiarity. Be available to your guests for helpful advice.
★ Never speak to your guests about your personal problems or concerns. Your guests have sometimes come away to

have a break from their problems – never burden them with yours.

To avoid any possible embarrassment to either party you should follow a few simple and easy rules:

★ Always knock on the door and wait for an answer. If after twenty seconds there is no reply, knock again. If again there's no answer you should call out a greeting 'Good morning/afternoon' and enter the room. If you are there to clean the room and your guests are still there, ask them if they wish you to come back later.

★ Don't ever knock on a room that has a 'Do not disturb' sign displayed. It is a good idea to provide these in all rooms for your guests' use – it helps gives you a signal as to whether or not they wish to be disturbed.

★ Some holiday lets/B&Bs advise their guests that the host's normal procedure is to stay out of their room unless the guest has a specific need that requires someone to go in there.

ANECDOTE: I was made aware of the embarrassing situation that occurred to a B&B host who offered a honeymoon suite. The young couple had booked in and had not been seen for some time! The host needed to access the room and followed the normal protocols for entry to a guest's room. However, the couple had not heard the many knocks on the door or the host's greeting, so the host entered, only to be confronted by a scene he would rather not have witnessed! Needless to say, he made a hasty retreat!

GUEST BEHAVIOUR

You have some rights here if your holiday let/B&B is also your home. You have the right to set some rules, such as how much alcohol can be consumed, noise levels, etc. How you monitor this, and to what length you wish to go, is a more difficult question. The main reason you may want to comment on a guest's behaviour is if it is disturbing you or other guests, if you suspect damage to your property, or if you suspect some illegal activity is occurring.

If you have to confront your guests about their *behaviour*, you should observe the following points:

★ Do so in person, and in private. If the problem is occurring in the guest bedroom, approach your guest there. Don't enter the room, but conduct your conversation at the door.
★ Try not to sound judgemental. Instead, gently advise your guest of the nature of the complaint and the suggested behaviour. Thank them for their time and excuse yourself.
★ If the guest's behaviour does not improve, you need to follow up your concern with the guest. Explain to the guest that it is your policy that the comfort of the household is paramount, and that one individual guest cannot disturb the peace of others. Ask for the guest to show consideration to their fellow guests. In most cases this will be enough; however, in rare cases you may have to ask the guest to leave.
★ If they refuse, you will need to contact the police. If you face the unhappy experience of this happening, you need to ensure that you are discreet in your handling of the affair, and keep the disturbance of any other guest to a minimum.
★ If you find damage to your property, you need to contact your online reservation platform, as most of these have a damage policy. Make a report of it as soon as you realise there is a problem.

NEIGHBOURS

Your neighbours' feelings about your holiday-let venture are going to be key to your success. They are going to be near you every day of the year, not just during the fleeting stays of your visitors. They are not getting any financial benefit from your venture so you need to ensure that you minimise any impact on them.

There are two things you can do to make this relationship easier:

★ Make sure that your guests are aware of any rights of way and do not block your neighbours' access.

★ Try to ensure that you follow disturbance rules regarding noise.

> ANECDOTE: One real estate company we know of had a complaint lodged by a neighbour of one of their tenants. The neighbour had noticed many people were coming and going next door at all hours of the day and night and were causing a disturbance. On further inspection it was discovered that the lessee had listed the property with a reservation platform – this contravened the terms of the lease, resulting in the tenants being evicted.

COMPLAINTS

Occasionally, you are going to have a customer who believes your best is not good enough. You need to use these complaints to your advantage; they are valuable feedback, which will enable you to refine your product. You will find that very few people will complain, but if you investigate you may find that other guests feel the same way. Every complaint will be different, but you need to ensure that your establishment has a procedure for dealing with complaints which everyone understands. A correctly handled complaint can actually increase goodwill in your business. Following are some guidelines you should consider in your handling of complaints.

Apologise

A statement like 'I am sorry you feel that way' does not admit fault but acknowledges your guest's feelings. Do not make excuses or trivialise the complaint. The customer only wants to know you are taking the grievance seriously. Avoid being drawn into a right and wrong argument. *Even if you win the argument, you will end up the loser if you make the guest feel trivialised.*

Never Patronise or Humiliate a Guest

This can have disastrous results, and in the event that the mistake was yours or a member of your staff's, you will be the one who will be humiliated.

FOLLOW-UP

Ensure that your guest was happy with your decision. Sometimes we believe we have settled a matter appropriately, only to find out, too late, that the guest was not at all happy. You must clarify the situation for mutual satisfaction.

ANECDOTE: Last year in Australia a woman let her property short term to another woman who used it for the duration as a makeshift brothel! Enough said!!

THE IMPORTANCE OF FEEDBACK

As we have said before, feedback, both positive and negative, can be the most important tool in the ongoing success of your business. Most guests won't express dissatisfaction directly to you, but would be most happy to fill in a *questionnaire*.

You can leave the questionnaire in the bedroom, accompanied by a thank-you letter and a stamped, self-addressed envelope. Your guest is given the option of leaving the questionnaire or posting it, or sending it by email after their stay. This action will demonstrate that you are interested in their considered comments.

The reservation platform that sent you the booking will ask guests to rate you out of five. As these ratings will go 'live', it is in your best interest to ensure that as far as possible you do all you can to ensure positive reviews.

ANECDOTE: I've been made aware of B&Bs and holiday lets that produce a quarterly newsletter and email it to their previous guests. The newsletter highlights attractions coming up in the area. This has resulted in a significant number of extra bookings for all the properties that provide this service.

SAFETY ISSUES

It is your duty to yourself, your family, your employees and your guests to provide a safe place in which to live, work and stay. To help facilitate this we suggest you set down a few guidelines that will cover fire safety, work practices and general instructions for guests.

Leave your reservation diary near the door at night so you can easily check everyone off and ensure all are safe.

Never deadlock your door while you or guests are inside. In the case of a fire, you may not be able to escape.

MAKING YOUR HOLIDAY LET/B&B A SAFE PLACE TO STAY

Room by room, you need to establish that your house is as safe as it can possibly be.

In the *bathrooms* you need to ensure that bath mats have non-stick backing, that the room is thoroughly disinfected after each guest's visit, that guests do not share bar soap and that no medication is kept in the bathroom. You might want to consider handrails near the bath and the shower.

The *kitchen* can be a hotbed for germs. You need to keep pets out of the kitchen and any dining areas. Any detergents and cleaning agents should be kept in a cupboard separate from food. Ensure you know how to treat poisoning that can occur from oral or eye contact with any of these agents. You should neither smoke nor eat when preparing food. Use separate cutting boards for meat and vegetables – label them accordingly, generally green for vegetables and red for meat. Keep fridge temperatures at five degrees Celsius. Cover any wounds with good-quality plasters and wear gloves both for cooking and cleaning, having separate gloves for each activity. Ensure you reheat foods thoroughly.

MAKING YOUR HOLIDAY LET/B&B A SAFE PLACE TO WORK

Not only should your holiday let be a safe place to stay; you also need to ensure it is a safe place to work. Train your staff and your family on fire procedures and how to use extinguishers and smother blankets. Have quarterly evacuations to ensure that everyone knows where the outside meeting point is.

Another safety precaution would be Hepatitis B vaccinations. Hepatitis is a rapidly spreading disease in all its permutations. As you are handling both food and cleaning, it might be a good investment to have this done. See your local doctor for his advice.

Wear clean clothes and rubber-based shoes when cleaning, as you don't want to spread germs. The most important thing you can wear when you clean, however, is a pair of gloves. It will protect you from all of the bacteria that you will encounter. Use different gloves for cleaning bathrooms than you would for cleaning any other room in the house. Do not touch your face with these gloves – ever.

SAFETY IN THE KITCHEN

Safety in the kitchen is twofold. It is about protecting you from accidents, in the most accident-prone place in your house, and protecting you and your guests from diseases, the obvious one being food poisoning. This can be avoided by the correct storage and cooking of food.

Although most online reservation platforms are not currently subjected to local council regulations, it is worth considering undertaking a *food-handling course* at your nearest accredited learning facility. This will give you legal status in some jurisdictions, especially if the course is accredited, in the event of accidents involving food and food handling. If it is not compulsory in your area, we would recommend you consider one of the recognised courses. They normally only last one or two days and can save you and your business a lot of anguish in the long run. They will teach you about effective hygiene practices, food storage, cleaning and sanitising, avoiding food contamination, food legislation and understanding legal obligations.

Using common sense and adhering to regulations, you will have fewer incidents of food-borne illness and lower associated medical costs. As a result, there will be increased consumer confidence, with the potential of positive word-of-mouth recommendations. Other industry sectors, such as tourism and the providers of food, will benefit from your diligence. In particular:

Identify the hazards: Some hazards can be controlled, while others may be beyond our control. For example, the quality of raw materials you receive is the responsibility of your suppliers, but you can control the storage and cooking process.

Identify the critical control points: These are the points at which important processes can go wrong. The difference between a Critical Control Point (CCP) and a hazard is that a CCP can be controlled and monitored. Temperature control in chillers and cold-rooms is a good example of a CCP.

PROVIDING FIRST AID

We believe you have a moral, if not legal, obligation to be able to provide *first aid* to your staff and guests in large establishments. One member of your staff or family being certified is probably enough, but it should be the person who is primarily running the establishment. Everyone in the household should know and understand your establishment's procedures for handling an emergency.

One thing you must do is purchase a comprehensive first aid kit. You need to maintain this kit and log any incidents that occur. Again, you can purchase this on the web through St John's Ambulance or a similar entity.

ANECDOTE: Wear good-quality gloves when making a bed. It has come to our attention that a host recently found a syringe in the bedding and it is not unknown to find used condoms.

CHAPTER 8

Food and the B&B

*We now reach the breakfast part of the B&B –
increasingly also offered by holiday lets. What are
you going to do about breakfast? Here you have
several options.*

THE FULLY COOKED OR CONTINENTAL BREAKFAST

In traditional B&Bs this is your opportunity to shine even if you are only providing a very simple breakfast. Breakfast is the meal your guests have been waiting for.

Start with the basics: a few cereals, fresh fruit juice, fruit compote or fruit, freshly baked bread, conserves, speciality teas and brewed coffee. Muffins and croissants are a nice extra.

Your guests may not want all of the above, but it should be on offer. What many will want is a hot meal and something different from what they would prepare at home. Our suggestion is that you offer a few different options for the guest to choose from. If your establishment is a self-catering Airbnb, the ingredients for a cooked breakfast can be provided.

A recent survey indicated that 95 per cent of people enjoyed a cooked breakfast, but 94 per cent only rarely ate one. However, when many people go on holiday they like to start the day with a cooked breakfast, so be prepared to oblige. Consider having one or two special dishes available every day and to rotate them, so that guests who are staying more than one night have some variety. There are great recipes available: e.g. eggs Benedict served on muffins with smoked salmon.

Having staples such as bacon, eggs, mushrooms and tomatoes in your cupboard will serve you well for those guests who prefer the more traditional fare.

As for quantity, you don't want to scrimp. Most guests won't be greedy, but they will want a hearty breakfast. The one disadvantage of having breakfast in your type of accommodation is that some guests will feel they should be able to eat as much as possible. You will need to factor this into your room rate/tariff.

Presentation is almost as important as the food itself. Whether serving your breakfast yourself or providing ingredients, you need to look at the aesthetic appearance of the food through the eyes of a paying guest. Take into account colour, texture and smell. The appreciation of food is through all five senses, so you should ensure you consider all of them when providing your meal.

These days there are any number of providers who supply free-range and organic products and who make wonderful sausages. These people often ensure delivery almost anywhere.

Remember, the room rate that you charge covers the night's stay plus the cost of a cooked breakfast, whether your guests have it or not. Any other service is an additional charge. If you offer items to your guests that are not covered by the online reservation platform – e.g. provision of a picnic lunch or a dinner – then you need to establish a method of payment. Don't forget to mention this on your reservation site.

For holiday lets that provide breakfast it is usually the *continental breakfast* traditionally consisting of a croissant or Danish pastry with coffee or tea, and, if you are lucky, a glass of juice. Some establishments are offering 'continental breakfast', but are actually providing fruit, toast, tea and coffee. As said before, these options need to be made clear in the description of your holiday let/B&B. Some guests desire a lighter meal and would be happy with a simple option.

THE BREAKFAST BASKET

The provision of a *breakfast basket* is popular with those guests who want to be out and about early; for example, walkers and cyclists. This is often the case in self-contained accommodation such as cabins on a farmstay, and for those staying in self-catering accommodation. It can contain fresh juice, fresh fruit compotes with yoghurt, freshly baked bread with jams and conserves, butter, a thermos of tea or coffee and often freshly baked goods such as Danish pastries and muffins, and the appropriate eating and drinking utensils. When there are cooking facilities, you can also supply bacon, eggs or freshly made speciality sausages.

Make your basket look like a gift to the guest.

OFFERING LUNCH

It is really up to you whether you offer *lunch,* and very few guests will expect it. If you do offer it, do so at an extra cost. Remember that preparing lunch for your guests will really break into your day. The amount you charge will never make up for the time you will have to spend preparing it.

A *picnic basket,* provided at an extra cost, is a popular option for the guests. This, as with the breakfast basket, is particularly popular in areas where people are likely to explore the natural wonders of the surrounding area. Preparation time is much the same as for an in-house lunch, but there is little cleaning up afterwards.

ALCOHOL LICENSING

Each country/state/local authority has its own Alcohol Licensing Act. Obtain a copy of it so that you are familiar with any legal implications associated with providing or allowing alcohol on your premises.

MORNING COFFEE AND AFTERNOON TEA

It is a great idea to welcome your travel-weary guests with *morning coffee or afternoon tea.* The traditional version of this is tea or coffee with home-baked goodies, such as scones or pikelets. Some accommodation providers are experimenting here as well. They are welcoming their guests with cheese, dips and antipasto. The only drawback with this is that it doesn't fill your house with the same aroma as freshly baked biscuits. As already mentioned, this is a great opportunity to catch up with your guests, find out their plans and give them some advice on your locality. You can use the opportunity to set down any house rules you might have and acquaint them with your fire escapes, etc.

If you have a large establishment, you could provide a High Tea, with dainty sandwiches and cakes, scones, a selection of wonderful teas and coffees, and even the occasional string quartet. In this way you could add some theatre to your establishment and earn some extra money, making it an open house.

EATING WITH GUESTS

We don't suggest you eat with guests, especially at breakfast. This, though, is really up to you and your guests. Breakfast is quite a difficult meal to serve and eat at the same time. You will also find your guests will sleep in and you will need your strength for the day ahead. Concerning international guests, Australians tend to be a bit shy at breakfast, so let them have this meal to themselves.

I have found that many guests are frequently rather uncomfortable sharing breakfast tables with each other, tending to be a bit monosyllabic and uncommunicative. You might find it better to ensure you have a few separate tables where couples can have breakfast 'alone'. Ask them for their seating preference the evening before.

If you are serving dinner, there is no reason why you should not eat with your guests. It is quite likely that if your guests have chosen to eat in, they would like some company. Don't overpower the conversation, but feel free to let your natural personality shine.

SELF-CONTAINED PROPERTIES

Many holiday lets are self-contained cottages with all the cooking facilities available for the guests' use. They typically expect to bring their own food unless otherwise informed.

KNOWING THE RESTAURANTS IN YOUR AREA

You need to become an expert on the pubs, clubs, cafes and restaurants in your area. These are some of the most important recommendations you will be asked to give. You need to have tried the restaurants you recommend because, like it or not, you will be judged on the quality of your recommendation.

You may be able to arrange a 10 per cent discount for your guests, or a free cup of coffee, or even a free meal for you and your partner, for every ten recommendations you send their way. Never enter into an arrangement such as this, however, unless you really believe the restaurant is up to scratch. A 'free' dinner for you is no reason to destroy your credibility. Your reputation is worth much more than that.

CHAPTER 9

Daily Operations

Your guests are here. You have your people skills off pat. You have established a business model that works for you. What you now need to do is look at the best way to run your business day to day. You need to establish systems that will allow you to enjoy your new lifestyle, and provide your guests with a fantastic holiday experience.
....

BOOKINGS

An earlier chapter discussed the things you will need to communicate to prospective guests over the phone or the Internet. What is now needed is to consider the *bookings* themselves, specifically how you are going to record them.

For those of you starting your own small accommodation enterprise, a *diary* is a good place to start. Divide each day into the number of rooms you have available. As you take bookings, you should record the following information in the appropriate space: the date you took the booking, the arrival and departure dates of your guest, the guest's name, address and phone number, and deposit information. If this is an Airbnb booking, they will email you concerning availability, as do most other global online reservation platforms. This still needs to be entered into your diary, as a diary is portable and can be referred to if you receive a booking enquiry when away from your property. Any comments, such as particular dietary requirements, estimated time of arrival, etc., will be entered into your diary as well.

Another good idea is to set up a *reservation chart* at the front of the diary, or on the wall of your office, near your phone. This chart will help you see at a glance if you have rooms free on a requested date.

With both the chart and the diary it is a good idea to make your reservations in pencil, in case alterations are needed.

Don't forget to block out days on the chart and in the diary when you will not be taking guests. For later reference, place the reason next to these 'time off' days; for example, holidays, family time, repairs, maintenance, etc.

> ANECDOTE: At the time of my writing this book, Airbnb say that they connect people at any price point, in more than 34,000 cities and 190 countries, and are processing multi-million guest bookings worldwide.

GUEST REGISTRATION

Although you may not need a guest register if you are taking bookings through a reservation platform, for your own reference it would be a good idea to keep one so that you know at a glance your booking availability dates.

Up until a few years ago an exercise book was sufficient for this purpose, but every year the level of professionalism in this industry is rising and it is this professionalism your guests will remember. They don't necessarily want to check in as if they were staying in a hotel, but an old exercise book is not really good enough.

So what are the options? There are two main forms of *registration*. One is the use of a *guest register* and the other is the individual *registration form* or card.

What Do You Need to Record?

Soon after your guests arrive, you may need to ensure that you have the following guest information for your records: full name, address and nationality, plus their passport number, country of origin, arrival and departure times, along with next destination point. (Diplomats do not need to register.) These records should be kept for legal reasons. A solicitor can advise you on the length of time you're required to keep these.

Guest Register

A guest register is a bound book, divided into columns, which your guests fill in upon arrival. Guests from overseas may need to fill out the country of residence, and passport number, and in some cases their next destination. In this situation you will need to sight your guest's passport.

The guest register is popular because all the details are in one place and in chronological order, making it easy for referral, and it is very inexpensive as each guest only takes up one line in the register. The downsides are that it can become tatty from overuse, illegible if guests make mistakes, and indiscreet, as your guests can easily see the personal details of other guests.

In some regions there is a legal requirement for larger establishments to keep a record of the full name and nationality of all guests over a certain age; in some regions, for example, it is sixteen years. Records in this instance must be kept for a minimum amount of time according to the area you live in. We suggest you contact your local authority for the legal requirements in your area.

Individual Registration Form or Card

The *individual registration card* performs the same functions as a register. It is more expensive than a register as each guest has an individual card; however, you can generate these forms easily on your computer. This format is discreet, as no one sees the form except you and your guest. It is neat; if a guest makes a mistake you can provide a new one and it can be filed easily. It also has space for both you and your guest to make comments (dietary, special needs, etc.), which can be valuable information for later visits.

INSURANCE

Regardless of whether your business is in your home, on your property, around the corner, leased by you or a variation on these themes, insurance is one of the most important considerations you will have when running your holiday let/B&B. It has the potential to protect your home and lifestyle in a way nothing else can – against the unexpected!

Insurance is a very simple concept. For an annual payment, an insurance company agrees to provide specific cover for your *building and contents and other holiday-let/B&B specific areas, including liability to your paying guests*. Many insurers provide the facility to spread payments by direct debit. There is likely to be a charge for this.

Even if you believe you have adequate funds to replace or repair any loss that could occur, consideration must be given to investing in a suitable insurance policy.

In fact, in our increasingly litigious and varied society it would be irresponsible not to be adequately insured. Remember, as a host, you have a responsibility not only to yourself and your family, but also to your guests.

So what constitutes adequate insurance in your specific case? Remember that one of the beauties of holiday lets/B&Bs is that you are all different from each other. Let us identify and evaluate the major areas of risk.

The biggest risk may in fact be the general public themselves.

You have people coming to your home or property whom you do not know and who do not know you. You have no idea how well or otherwise they look after their own possessions, so how can you know how they will look after yours?

Most holiday-let/B&B guests are the loveliest of people and some become lifelong friends. Some, however, you will never please and you will wonder why they came in the first place. Things get broken perhaps, but no one confesses. Perhaps your lovely bathrobes disappear after the guests leave. How do you handle situations like this and remain hospitable and content?

What Cover Do I Need to Consider?
PUBLIC LIABILITY
Public liability relates to the general public in a business sense. It relates to injury and property damage caused by your alleged personal negligence and/or business negligence. If part of your property is not well maintained and clear of debris, a guest may fall and sustain an injury. Where you are proven to have been negligent, the cost of defending such claims is covered.

Product liability is in relation to any products you provide, but especially relevant to the food you serve. It doesn't matter whether you bought it from the bakery or not; should a guest find something 'extra' in it, you are liable.

ANECDOTE: There was a case many years ago when a guest found part of a cockroach in her slice of toast. She successfully sued and received a payout. Fortunately, the accommodation provider was insured for such mishaps.

Some reservation platforms have a one million US dollar guest damage policy that covers you in the event of any damage caused by guests. This will be converted into local currency as applicable.

Another policy to consider if applicable is *Employers Liability* – once you know that you are going to employ staff, be they full-time, part-time or casual cleaners, chefs or gardeners, talk with your insurance broker in detail about Employers Liability insurance. This is compulsory in the UK and may be automatically covered by your home insurance.

POINTS OF INTEREST
When assessing your contents cover, have special regard for antiques, valuables and other high-risk portable items such as cameras, laptops and jewellery. Some insurers may ask you to improve the security of your home (for example, by fitting a safe) if these items form a high proportion of your overall cover. It is often a requirement that you collate a list of these and keep photographic evidence and receipts. This proves to the insurer that you actually owned these items, and it also verifies their value.

ALTERNATIVE ACCOMMODATION AND RENT
This is likely to be a benefit of a specialist holiday-let/B&B policy. It will cover the additional costs you incur for alternative accommodation while your home is uninhabitable following a major loss. The amount of cover provided is usually expressed as a percentage of the contents sum insured.

Insurers will still have differences between the coverage they offer and their service and involvement in the industry, but it will be specific to the Small Accommodation Industry. Don't be afraid to get different quotes and ask as many questions as you can. This allows you to make educated decisions and buy as directly as possible.

Important note: The running of a commercial operation from the domestic residence is something that needs to be disclosed to the insurer of a Domestic Home and Contents policy. It is up to that insurer to determine how they will consider the impact of that business with regards to the risk. All insurers will have a different view. As the risk is no longer deemed purely 'domestic', it is a change in the materiality of the risk, and therefore, under the Duty of Disclosure owed by a policy holder, they are compelled to advise their insurer of this change.

KEEPING FINANCIAL RECORDS

You need to keep records of your holiday let/B&B's financial performance primarily for taxation purposes, but also to help monitor your business's growth. *VAT/GST records* are required to be kept by all registered business operators. As already mentioned many times in this publication, it would be wise to contact a financial advisor prior to deciding on anything to do with your establishment. The Inland Revenue Office, particularly, is a font of information. You are legally required to keep your records for taxation purposes, and the Tax Office has a CD-ROM designed for this purpose.

Sage, MYOB, Quickbooks or a similar computer record-keeping program is another worthwhile investment for record keeping and for tracking your business activities, especially if you are a larger accommodation provider. Due to the complexities of tax systems, there isn't room here to go into depth on the records the government requires you to keep.

As for the figures you need to assess your financial progress, it's a good idea to reconcile these each month and look at the following:

Accommodation Cash Flow

This is the permanent record of your occupancy and income. With this information you can compare month-to-month, year-to-year trading, highlighting regular seasonal highs and lows and allowing you to forecast accurately. You can then turn this information into graphs, perhaps even comparing weekend and weekday trade, to plan for the coming year or season. As months go by you will be able to make decisions on when your busiest periods are, thus enabling you to promote your property at times that suit you. This will enable you to make time for yourself to take a well-earned break.

If you are using your property's income to save for a specific event, it is important to monitor this income so that you know how long it will take to reach your target.

If your guest booking is via Airbnb then payment for the total amount minus their 3 per cent commission is deposited into your account twenty-four hours after the guests have departed.

ANECDOTE: Many holiday-let/B&B hosts in the past have accepted foreign currency as payment and to their horror found that the exchange rate was against them. There are often hidden charges with foreign exchange that you may not be aware of. Cash in your country's currency is best, if possible!

HOUSEKEEPING

Housekeeping is the centrepiece of successful holiday-let/B&B operation. Any existing host will tell you that *if you are not a committed housekeeper, then this form of accommodation provision is not for you.*

You will have to be a fanatical cleaner always, with an eye open for that lone hair in the shower or the wad of dust under the bed. Are you one of those people where everything has a place? Do you regularly clean under the beds? Do you lift all your ornaments up and individually wipe them and the surface beneath them every time you clean? And do you clean around plugholes with a toothbrush? Does your house have the air of a magazine layout?

If you do the above then you are the sort of person who should run a holiday let/B&B. You can never be too clean when operating this type of establishment. Cleanliness that is good enough for friends and family may not be good enough for paying guests. The two things that will destroy your reputation as a host are bad beds, and therefore a bad night's sleep, and the perception that your house is dirty.

Even though your guest has chosen this form of accommodation for its 'homely' atmosphere, what they actually want is the picture-book version of home. They want everything to be spotlessly clean and sparkling. This will put them in a happy mood and make them feel relaxed.

BEING PREPARED

When getting ready to clean, ensure that you are suitably attired. As emphasised earlier, wear flat, rubber-soled shoes, an apron and gloves. Be very careful when emptying rubbish bins and when cleaning generally, as you do not know what people might leave behind. Have all your products together in an easy-to-transport container.

Having a cupboard in your laundry designated for cleaning products is a good idea. Ensure that you know what chemicals are in each product and the treatment in the event of accidental poisoning.

A CLEANING CHECKLIST

It is a good idea to create a *checklist* for cleaning each room. This will serve as a reminder that you have covered everything when setting up for your guest, and as a guide for any outside help.

TAKING CARE OF YOUR FURNITURE

You need to remember that your furniture will be used by your guests. They, however, may not take as good care of it as you would. Thus, it becomes your responsibility to take care of it sufficiently for all of you.

★ Provide table mats and plenty of coasters on coffee tables, bedside tables, lamp tables, etc. and encourage guests to use them.
★ Wipe furniture daily.
★ Have your couches professionally cleaned regularly.

★ A good cleaning fluid does wonders on most surfaces, including granite. Many marks can be moved by one tablespoon of vinegar to a litre of water.

★ Keep paths free from weeds and overgrown plants, and remove and replace plants as need dictates. Gardens need to be tended and your guests will appreciate the care you take of their sanctuary (and yours)! Make sure you check for cobwebs!

★ Check outdoor lighting nightly to ensure the bulbs are functioning.

CHAPTER 10

Joining the Hospitality Industry

The important thing to remember as you start this journey is that you are not alone. You are part of a larger entity called the hospitality industry. Much of your success will depend on your ability to work co-operatively with others in the industry, both here and overseas.

·························

Many of those who list with an online reservation platform have bypassed their local tourist body. The reliance on one area of tourism may work in the short term, but it is wise to keep ahead of the game. Here, your local tourist body will be invaluable.

THE STRUCTURE OF TOURISM AUTHORITIES

There are state/country National Tourism Boards which, in essence, take responsibility for the developing strategies that ensure their share of tourist revenue. If the tourist authorities do not have successful marketing strategies based on the needs of their area, then they may not be receiving the maximum number of visits or, therefore, the highest possible revenue.

It is worth considering joining your B&B association, as it links you to your peer group. We encourage everyone in the holiday-let industry to join their local tourism organisation, board or association (in some places, a form of membership is compulsory). This will help you to identify why tourists visit your area, to network with other small accommodation operators, to access local information that helps you make better target market decisions, and to keep you up to date with tourism development. Be proactive, not reactive.

LOCAL TOURIST ORGANISATIONS

If you have not yet got the picture that you should consider being actively involved in the tourism community, even on a casual basis, this book has failed. Your local tourism authority is probably the most important organisation you can be in touch with. It will provide you with vital information about your market, but most importantly it will give you vital contacts. Local tourism operators thrive on interaction with each other. It really is a case of 'you scratch my back and I'll scratch yours'.

BED AND BREAKFAST ASSOCIATIONS

B&B associations are set up as advisory organisations on their members' behalf and subsequently cover current trends and regulations that have an impact on the B&B accommodation industry. They make up your peer group and are invaluable for networking on many levels.

DESTINATION MARKETING

Destination marketing plays an integral part in the marketing of tourism products. Whether the product is an attraction, activity, scenery or a holiday let/B&B, they all, collectively, form the essence of the destination. The more popular the destination, the better are the chances for individual tourism operators to promote and sell their products to potential customers in a cost-effective way.

Destination marketing, promoting the unique brand of a destination, is one of the tasks local or regional tourism organisations are charged with. They prepare the base from which individual operators can undertake their own marketing and promotion at a reduced cost.

Locations such as the Blue Mountains or the Painted Desert may not mean a lot to many people, nor would they necessarily associate them with any type of holiday experience. Mention the destination brand Tuscany, and the story is different. Many will not only associate that brand with a very specific holiday expectation, but can also place it geographically. In other words, if the destination is known in the marketplace or if it has brand identity, each business within it has the chance of being seen in its marketplace and to reach potential customers faster and at a reduced cost.

It should be in everyone's interest, from the smallest accommodation operator to the largest attraction, to ensure that your local and regional tourism organisations receive sufficient support to undertake destination marketing, promote the region and create brand awareness. In return, individual businesses will benefit.

OFFICIAL STAR GRADING DEFINITIONS

Recognised star grading systems allow for a third party to grade your property. This has more credibility than other options.

Definitions of the prime categories set down by the grading authorities are as follows:

Bed & Breakfast   Accommodation in a private house, run by the owner and having a limited number of guestrooms, generally up to five.

Guesthouse   Accommodation provided for a larger number of guests than a traditional B&B and run on a more commercial basis than a B&B. Usually offers more services; e.g. dinner provided by the owners.

Farmstay   B&B or guesthouse accommodation provided on a working farm or smallholding.

Self-contained cottages can also be graded.

STATUTORY OBLIGATIONS

With the grading of a property come statutory obligations that must be adhered to. They include the following:

fire precautions;

price display orders;

food safety;

hygiene;

licensing;

Health and Safety;

anti-discrimination.

GRADING

It is a good idea to choose a recognised grading organisation, click onto their website and download the PDF file on their grading format. Analyse how it would impact on the way you prepare your property for holiday-let/B&B purposes.

So why should you be classified? As more people enter this market the guest is going to become more discerning. Those properties that can advertise their rating will only benefit from it.

Tourism accreditation is a process designed to establish and continually improve industry standards for conducting tourism businesses. It aims to assist every tourism business to improve the way it operates. Given that the system is third-party graded, it has considerable credibility.

It is important to bear in mind that the star grading system takes into account the nature of the property and the expectation of the guests – so a farmhouse is just as entitled to five stars as a country hotel, as long as what it offers is of the highest standard and satisfies all the grading parameters.

★	Fair and acceptable
★★	Good
★★★	Very good
★★★★	Excellent
★★★★★	Exceptional, world-class

This rating system of one to five stars offers the best way for guests to assess the potential quality of a stay at a particular property. Ratings are an internationally applied yardstick and are administered in each country according to very strict guidelines. These ratings can appear on your property's description section, as seen on the Airbnb reservation site and other similar sites.

ANECDOTE: Many of those who run B&Bs have realised that they can better justify their room rate if they are star rated. A long-time operator in our area found that once their farm was star rated the bookings increased substantially.

FEASIBILITY STUDY

If you are a large or small enterprise, completing your feasibility study enables you to test the viability of your business proposition before committing sums of money to a venture that may well fail.

Remember that your property will not appeal to everybody and that you should be identifying the type of guests you want to attract, i.e. your preferred target market.

Apart from just listing your property on Airbnb, TripAdvisor, Wimdu, Booking.com, Expedia and others, who will send you potential bookings from all different kinds of people, ask yourself what type of guests you would like to attract to your property? The choice is yours – you should make this decision at an early stage. Would you prefer to be servicing the top of the market or the no-frills sector? Would you feel more comfortable with corporate clients or with family groups? Your choice of target market will be a vital factor in influencing your decision on where to locate and how to design your premises. If, on the other hand, you decide to use your existing dwelling with modifications, then you must determine what type of guest your property will attract. Your property will dictate the direction you take.

Having identified your preferred market groups (this can also indicate age and income), you can now determine whether your property is in the right location to meet your selected market or whether you need to consider changing your target market.

CREATING A FINANCIAL MODEL

It is vital to separate your family and your business financial requirements and keep these as separate entities. This will assist you in recognising the facilities you will need for your family as separate from those of your business. At the start of creating a financial model it is important to know what times throughout the year you want to host guests. Once this is decided, you can then start to calculate the number of room nights multiplied by the room rate.

Let us assume that your proposed room rate is £100/€100/$100 per night and that you have three guestrooms, all with their own en-suites, and priced the same.

Let us also assume that in the first operating year your occupancy rate is targeted at 40 per cent. That means there are approximately twenty-one weeks of projected bookings, which represents 146 days × three guestrooms equals 438 room nights. If every booking was worth £100/€100/$100, then the annual *turnover* would be £43,800/€43,800/$43,800.

> ANECDOTE: Remember the old adage: you have to spend money to make money. Doing things on the cheap is usually a waste of your hard-earned savings. This reminds me of the couple who spent a considerable sum readying their new premises for a B&B designed to run cooking classes. They attended several relevant courses themselves and networked extensively among the B&B and cooking fraternity. Due to their diligent research it was only a short time before they were making a profit and could start to recoup their expenditure.

CHAPTER 11

Holiday Accommodation Marketing

The underpinning factor of your marketing concept rests on the importance of guests to your holiday destination. All of your activities should be aimed at satisfying your guests' needs, while obtaining a profitable, rather than maximum, occupancy.

DEVELOPING A MARKETING CONCEPT

To develop a marketing concept for your type of accommodation you must:

★ determine the needs of your guests (market research),
★ develop competitive advantages (marketing strategy),
★ select specific markets to serve (target marketing), and
★ determine how to satisfy those needs (marketing mix).

Even for a small establishment, these principles remain true. This avoids guesswork and a hit-and-miss approach to business. A rise in income can be exponentially in proportion to adhering to these principles.

DOING MARKET RESEARCH

The fundamentals of operating a successful holiday let/B&B are the same as in running any small business. If you do your homework first, there is less likelihood of coming unstuck later.

The aim of *market research* is to find out: who your guests are; what they want; where and when they want it.

This research can also expose problems in the way in which you provide products or services, and find areas for expansion of current services to fill customer demand.

Market research should also identify trends that can affect bookings and profit levels and should give you more information than simply who your customers are. Use this knowledge to determine matters such as your market share, the effectiveness of your advertising and promotions, and the response to any new value-added services that you have introduced.

While larger companies hire professionals to do their research, small business owners and managers are closer to their customers and are better able to learn much faster the likes and dislikes of their guests. They are better positioned to react quickly to any change in customer preferences.

Trends:

System changes; e.g. *the rise of the online reservation platform*.

Any population shifts.

Changes in local tourism development.

Lifestyle changes in the nearest inner-city area.

Short-break holidays taken during the week instead of only at weekends.

Market research does not have to be sophisticated and expensive. While money can be spent in collecting research material, a lot of valuable information can be accessed by the holiday-let/B&B operator using the following ideas.

Guests

Talk to your guests to get a feel for your clientele, and ask them where improvements can be made. Collecting guest comments and suggestions is an effective form of research, and it also instils customer confidence in your product and property.

Never discount a guest's comments, however often you may be confronted by them. Treat all comments as a learning experience.

Employees

If you have employees, even if only a cleaner once a week, this is one of the best sources of information about guests' likes and dislikes. Usually employees work more directly with guests and hear complaints that may not make it to the owner. They are also aware of items or services that guests may request, and that the holiday let/B&B doesn't currently offer.

COMPETITION

Monitoring the competition can be a useful source of information. Competitors' activities may provide important information about guest demands that you have overlooked. They may be capturing part of the market by offering something unique or different. Likewise, small accommodation providers can capitalise on unique points of their product that the competition does not offer.

Ask yourself the following:

What is the competition's market share?

How much revenue do you suspect they make?

How many holiday lets/B&Bs are targeting the same market?

What attracts customers to them?

What strengths do they advertise?

RECORDS AND FILES

Looking at your business records and files can be very informative. Peruse your revenue records, complaints, receipts or any other records that can show you where your guests live or work, or what interests them.

With this kind of information, you can cross-reference guest addresses and check the effectiveness of the advertising placements. You need to take into account that this material was produced in the past, so may be obsolete now, but at least you will have a general idea of what to look for.

You can use this information to generate a pithy comment to include on your reservation platform. For example, you might have an outdoor area that offers beautiful views of the countryside.

ANECDOTE: One holiday-let operator found that addresses on cash receipts allowed for the pinpointing of guests in a specific geographic area. She thought clients might like to sample the similar, yet different, features her area offered. As an enhancement she also put together packages with local tourist providers. This was to appeal to guests who live in a specific area; for example, those who live in a rural setting on the coast who might like to stay in a big city on the coast. They would still have the coastal lifestyle but with the advantage of all the amenities a big city offers. On putting this idea into action, she found that her occupancy rate and income increased dramatically.

DEVELOPING A MARKETING STRATEGY

With the research information gathered, the next step is to develop a marketing strategy. Use this information to determine areas in which the competition doesn't adequately fill consumer demand, or in which a new service or different promotion would capture part of the market. A new accommodation provider may capture a significant market share by aiming its marketing strategy at areas not focused on by the competition.

Some examples of possible areas include offering:

★ more innovative sight-seeing options,
★ better value for the guests, for example an emphasis on quality,
★ a specialised service instead of a broad one,
★ modified facilities, or any improvements you may need to make to your property, and
★ a flexible pricing policy.

While a new holiday let/B&B can enter this business and capture a share of the market, an established one can use the same strategies to increase its market share.

TARGET MARKETING

Once your marketing strategy is developed, you need to match this to your customer requirements to see if the strategy is workable. For example, a 'value for money' option may be appealing to the family market, while 'quality and top service' would be more attractive to couples.

Remember that different market strategies may appeal to different target markets. Apply the collected data to choose the combinations that will work best.

The market is defined by different segments. Some examples of this are:

Geographic

Specialised product options to suit guests who live in certain neighbourhoods or regions, or who are from different climates. For example, farm holidays can target city and town residents.

Demographic

Direct advertising to families, retired people, the disadvantaged, or aimed at potential guests of a particular occupation or profession.

Special Interest Groups

Target promotions to fit the opinions or attitudes of the customers; political or religious, for example.

Product Benefits

Aim marketing to appeal to those seeking particular benefits or features; for example, low cost or easy access.

Previous Guests

Identify possible special events or packages and promote these to guests who have stayed before.

THE MARKETING MIX

Before the marketing mix decision is made, determine what purpose these marketing efforts are going to serve. Are they to deepen the customer base; increase market share; increase revenue; reach new geographic markets; or increase occupancy?

After objectives are established, determine a date for accomplishing them. The marketing mix allows the holiday let/B&B to combine different marketing decision areas such as services, promotion and advertising, pricing and place, to construct an overall marketing programme.

PRODUCTS AND SERVICES

Use the product or service itself as a marketing resource. Having something unique provides material for your advertising. While the ideas mentioned under market strategy apply here, another option is to change or modify the service. Potential clients may pay extra attention to a product or service if it has been changed or enhanced in some way. Remember, sales and promotional opportunities are generated by product differentiation.

PROMOTION AND ADVERTISING

While you are listed with an online reservation platform you may still choose to do individual marketing. With a marketing strategy and clear objectives outlined, you can advertise and promote your product through: your telephone directory; a press release; the newspaper; holiday-let/B&B guide books; local tourism publications; Facebook and Twitter. Successful advertising has included such things as special bridal party deals, and theatre and dinner packages.

The Internet is a relatively cheap way to promote your property, both domestically and overseas, and should now be considered the centrepiece of your overall marketing strategy.

One reason to advertise is to highlight promotional activities. This will serve to both highlight your property and offer added incentive for customer patronage. For example, you may wish to promote midweek stays; two nights for the price of one; or special activities – e.g., tours with a local bus company – included in the price.

The *Four in a Bed* TV series – screened by Channel 4 in the United Kingdom – is worth considering entering. A B&B in North Yorkshire has been highly rated on TripAdvisor after winning the hit show. Similarly, Newton House B&B in Knaresborough took the honours after a week-long battle with three other contestants and has also been highly rated on TripAdvisor.

The aim of any small business is to try to reach the largest number of people through whatever money has been allocated to advertising and promotion. It can be worth using several different methods of advertising. Be creative and implement ideas.

PUBLIC RELATIONS

Public relations means the ability to make yourself known in the marketplace and in your locality in a friendly and professional manner. The way you relate to the travelling public is of critical importance in the small accommodation sector.

All holiday lets/B&Bs will have certain things in common: if nothing else, you are dealing with people who are away from their home. Understanding what this form of accommodation has to offer, and the people who patronise it, will play an important part in how you relate to your guests and in your marketing approach.

Typically, people frequent holiday lets/B&Bs for:

★ The personal, pampered feeling offered by traditional B&Bs and by some holiday lets.
★ The safety and security offered by smaller establishments.
★ The opportunity for closer interaction with local surroundings.
★ Their suitability for short holiday breaks.
★ Convenience – servicing their needs at the time.
★ Value for money.

Taking these factors into account, you could find that word of mouth offers your enterprise your cheapest and most effective form of promotion; it may thus be an important tool in your public relations outreach. Look at promoting not only yourself, but also the attractions of your area, offering your holiday let/B&B as the most convenient place to stay.

Media Releases

Following are some rules to observe when preparing a press release.

Write your story considering the questions, 'WHO, WHAT, WHY, WHEN, WHERE and HOW'. This will help you to include all relevant information.

You must remain focused on what your story is and ensure it is different from all the other media kits that appear on journalists' desks daily. Media kits are the material supplied by an organisation to set out their requirements; for example, all the information the publisher needs to run your story. Remember, if the story isn't clear to you, it won't be to the journalist or the readers.

Restrict your story to one A4-size page. Use your letterhead, as it contains your address and other contact details. Also include your contact name and phone number at the end of your story.

Your media release must be typed, with at least 1.5 line spacing. 'Publisher', a Microsoft program, comes with a format specifically for media releases.

Make your story clear and concise, using simple language. Have a short and punchy title. Do not exaggerate. Remember this may appear in print and you have to be able to deliver.

Pay attention to details such as dates and times.

Double-check your spelling. This attention to detail is seen as a basic courtesy by journalists.

Targeting Your Story

If the emphasis of your holiday let/B&B is on food, food sections of newspapers or gourmet magazines are naturally where your story is best suited. If you offer unique scenery, try the travel section of a weekend paper. If you have gardens that have won awards, then the home or gardening section could be an opportunity.

Prior to writing your release, read the sections of the paper/ magazine you are targeting carefully to understand what it is in each story that captured the imagination of the editor and made it topical.

Get to know your local papers, their deadlines and the names of staff you will be targeting. Being an active member of your community will enhance your chance of getting a media profile.

A week after posting your media kit, follow up with a phone call. Ask if the media kit has been received. If not, explain briefly what it is about and offer to send another copy. If the editor has seen it, ask them if they need more information and if they think the story is suitable.

Instead of a traditional media kit, you may consider offering journalists and their partners a first-hand experience of your accommodation. A free night's stay is a cheap price to pay for a glowing report in a popular magazine or in the travel section of a metropolitan newspaper. A journalist's visit will not necessarily guarantee you fantastic copy or even an article, but 'freebies' or 'familiarisations' for journalists are part of the system, and any positive word-of-mouth report their stay might generate will unquestionably be to your advantage.

For best effect, limit the period of the offer so that journalists are less likely to put it away and forget about you. Good editorial coverage may not make your business, but it can provide the icing on the cake of your marketing plan. Done well, it is economical and effective.

Public relations are also about relations with your local community. Build up positive relationships with local clubs and business organisations so that you and your business become known and trusted by the locals. Public relations may also include sponsoring a fundraising event or local sports team.

HOW MUCH MARKETING DO I NEED?

Any expenses incurred in promoting your business can be set against any tax you might pay on your profits; however, this can be complicated when you are first embarking upon your venture. Consult your accountant before spending any money. What you should not do is decide that you need a certain type of advertisement just because that's what everyone else does. You must decide what is appropriate to your holiday let/B&B at any given time. You should, however, have some idea about who it is you are trying to attract and how best to reach them.

A marketing plan and budget needs to be developed in conjunction with your business plan.

Marketing Plan

A marketing plan is especially relevant for larger accommodation providers and should outline your marketing goals for a twelve-month period. Parameters should be set as to how you expect to achieve these goals through advertising, promotion, marketing and public relations.

You should include the following elements:

★ tourist information centres
★ direct mail campaigns (including newsletters)
★ public relations (community and media activities)
★ advertising
★ brochure stationery
★ business stationery
★ group promotions
★ websites
★ trade and tourism shows
★ any other activity that will get your enterprise noticed by the public. Networking with other hosts may be the most important one.

Carefully consider any promotional or marketing schemes and opportunities offered to you by your local or regional tourism organisations. The benefits here can be considerable.

Your marketing plan will identify your target market and how you plan to reach it.

Do not forget your local community. Word of mouth is the best advertising for any business, especially smaller ones. Locals will continually be asked for their accommodation recommendations.

Joining your local Chamber of Commerce, Rotary or Lions Club, or other community organisation can bring benefits in the form of increased guest numbers and word-of-mouth promotion. Include membership fees, donations and sponsorships in your marketing plan budget.

Also allow for hidden costs such as photography, artwork design and production. A contingency of 12 per cent will allow for incidentals and price rises for the year.

NEWSLETTERS

Newsletters and leaflets are an effective way to communicate with your community and with past guests.

Microsoft Publisher has a number of template options that you can adapt for your holiday let/B&B. These are a great way to create a positive presence in your community and reinforce all the elements of your marketing plan. These newsletters and leaflets need not be expensive. You can design them on your computer, photocopy them, or even email them to your mailing list.

If you include interesting topics and amusing text, they may be passed on from friend to friend. You might want to have the occasional special offer to ascertain the effectiveness of your public relations. For example, you may want to include midweek specials – e.g. stay two nights and get the third one free of charge – to test your assumptions.

CHAPTER 12

Online Reservation Platforms

As already mentioned, there are several global online reservation platforms that encourage you to list your property on their websites; e.g. Airbnb, TripAdvisor, Wimdu, bookings.com and Expedia, to name a few. These services are popular with consumers. The sharing economy is changing the way in which people book their accommodation. Most global reservation systems list holiday lets under the B&B heading.

·······················

Remember that owners are still responsible for adhering to local authority regulations even though they are listed with global reservation systems.

If they do not adhere to local health and safety regulations, property owners place themselves at risk should anything go wrong while hosting guests; for example, personal accidents, inadequate public liability cover, and no, or limited, fire safety precautions.

The following information explains the essentials of how reservation platforms work and how you can list your property on their sites.

HOW ONLINE RESERVATION PLATFORMS WORK

All the online reservation platforms mentioned in this book work internationally, with some tending to operate at particular levels – for example, northern hemisphere, southern hemisphere etc. – for marketing purposes. Their websites allow people to book listed accommodation in all shown countries. They also allow the potential guest to access the site by desired postcode or town or city address.

The following are likely requirements, taken from a cross section of reservation platforms, for you to fill in when listing your property.

★ List property name.
★ Describe the property type you want listed; for example: B&B, cottage, apartment, self-contained, cave, train carriage, boat, to name a few.
★ How many people your property can accommodate and what city you are located in.
★ How many bedrooms and bed types.
★ How many bathrooms/en suites. Whether some are shared.
★ Children's activities, family friendly.
★ Breakfast included.
★ Kitchenette available for guests.
★ Room service.
★ Free high-speed Internet (Wi-Fi).
★ Pet friendly.
★ Wheelchair access.
★ Add photos of the guestrooms and property in general.
★ Set your pricing; i.e. room rate and or weekly/monthly rates.
★ Fill in safety card that lists fire emergency exits, phone numbers to call in case of fire, accident, police etc.
★ Availability.
★ If there is a minimum-stay requirement; for example, three nights or fewer.
★ Security: is it on site and what type?
★ Whether there are staff on site.
★ Housekeeping – is it included in the room rate?
★ Housekeeping frequency – daily, weekly, bi-weekly, none during any short stay.
★ Map locator indicating property whereabouts.
★ Airport transportation; is there a shuttle service?
★ Bar/lounge, beverage selection.
★ Restaurant or casino nearby.
★ Fitness centre or swimming pool.

ONLINE RESERVATION PLATFORM FEES AND COMMISSION STRUCTURES

Most online reservation platforms do not charge a listing fee but charge a commission ranging from 3 per cent to 15 per cent for bookings taken. Some also charge the customers a booking fee that ranges from 3 per cent to 6 per cent (depending on how many nights booked and/or the total price), while other operators might charge a set amount.

Some reservation platforms cover you for damage the guests might do to your property.

It is a very simple process to list your property; just follow the prompts shown on the reservation platform websites and you will be fine.

Payments for all bookings are normally processed and paid into your bank account twenty-four hours after guest arrival. When listing your property with a reservation platform, you will be advised of the exact timing of your payment.

Remember that reservation sites ask the departing guests to rate your property (1–5) and similarly encourage hosts to rate their guests (1–5).

Guest References

References are a good way to build rapport with potential guests. Word-of-mouth referrals and comments in the B&B guest book concerning the benefits of staying all offer excellent leverage in communicating with your guests. A reference can potentially increase the number of booking requests new owners receive.

HOW DO AIRBNB REFERENCES WORK?

Hosts and guests can receive public references from friends, family members and colleagues to help build their profile. References help people throughout the Airbnb community get to know you, and to feel more comfortable booking a reservation with you.

You need an Airbnb account to request and write references, and a reference will only display on the recipient's profile if the author of the reference has a profile photo of their own.

....

CHAPTER 13

Business Basics

....

CHOOSING A LEGAL STRUCTURE

Choosing the legal structure within which your business will trade is one of the first decisions you will need to make. You must discuss the best options for you with your solicitor and financial advisor.

To help you be armed for the meeting, a synopsis of your options follows. You must not make your final decision based on this, as each business's financial position is different and only your solicitor and your financial advisor have the tools to decide which structure best suits your situation.

It is worth noting at this point that you must be honest with your financial advisor and solicitor about your financial position. They will make decisions regarding your financial affairs based on the information you give them. If you withhold information it will only be to your financial detriment.

Sole Trader

The main advantage of being a sole trader is that you are your own boss. The profits are all yours, but so are the losses. You make all the decisions relating to the business yourself – something that can be both a positive and a negative. Tax breaks are usually not as generous. The main disadvantage is that you are personally liable for any business debts, which could put your personal assets at risk.

Partnership

A partnership requires two or more people. It works well for husband-and-wife teams. It has the advantage of pooling resources: financial, experience, brains. It also disperses the risk. Commonly cited disadvantages are disagreements over decision making and unequal distribution of work. A Partnership Agreement is an essential tool that will clarify from the outset the responsibilities of each partner. The time spent working this out at the beginning of the partnership minimises possible disagreements later. Your solicitor can help you draw up this agreement.

Company

A company is a separate entity from its shareholders and as such continues to exist when members change. It is created by incorporation under corporate law.

The company structure allows you to separate your personal activities from your business activities. Tax advantages are good, but you may still incur personal liability for the liabilities of the company.

Trusts

This is definitely a decision for your financial advisor. Trusts are administered by the trustee for the benefit of the beneficiaries of the trust. There are a few different types of trust and your financial advisor will best be able to advise you on their benefits.

BUSINESS NAMES

Be sure to register your business name – for example, Mount Tavy Cottage – so as to protect your investment, as no one else can register the same name.

So, what is a 'business name'? It is a name used by any person, partnership, company or trust for carrying on a business. It is advisable to consult a solicitor before using a business name. You should also check local phone books and any relevant trade journals or magazines, to see if any other business is already using the name. If it is, you could face legal difficulties.

SETTING YOUR ROOM RATE

Planning ahead, what should the room rate of your holiday let/B&B be in the first operating year?

I suggest that you take a 'calculated guess'. Let us assume, for the sake of this exercise, that your guess is £/€/$60 per night per room.

Look up a holiday letting guide and find two properties that already charge £/€/$60 per night and book yourself in for a short stay. Be sure that the two properties are located in a similar environment to yours, but not necessarily in the same locality. For example, if your property is a coastal one, find two others that are also located on the coast. While there, take the opportunity to check the level of hosting and facilities offered for £/€/$60 per night. You may find that one out of every three remarks in the visitors' book relates directly to the intrinsic beauty of the gardens. These comments may point to why the establishment is so popular.

After you have stayed in the two selected properties, revisit your own mental picture of your finished holiday let/B&B and you may find that what you are going to offer could attract a room rate of £/€/$70 per night or, conversely, £/€/$50 per night. In this way, you are going to make a more informed decision. Whatever you do, don't under-price or over-price your room rate.

Determining pricing levels and pricing policies is the major factor affecting revenue. Factors such as demand, the market price and customer responsiveness to price changes influence the price levels. Other factors, such as a convenient location or a more personalised service, may allow a holiday let/B&B owner to charge a higher room rate.

In some regions, accommodation that offers more than four guestrooms must display, in a prominent place, the minimum and maximum room rates that have been set.

TAX OBLIGATIONS
Capital Gains Tax

In some areas, when you sell a property you may have to pay capital gains tax (CGT). This may or may not be on the whole price you sell for, but may apply to the gain you make in selling it. Check this with your accountant.

GST/VAT

With GST/VAT, and any other value added tax, there is much your business will need to do to ensure it is compliant. The other concern for you in terms of taxation is that, in most cases, you are turning your family home into a business. *You will need very good taxation advice prior to taking in your first guest.* Make this a top priority.

SMARTPHONES

Smartphones have been with us long enough for people to consider them a natural extension of communication. A computer/smartphone, with connection to the Internet, extends all areas of audio, visual and written communication. It can be used (even adding video through webcam) for online communication in the form of email or texting, as well as for photographs, videos and live audiovisual connections. Many online reservation companies have apps that you can download onto your smartphone. The apps lists all of the provider's properties, so it's important that your holiday let/B&B's advertisement is concise and to the point.

THE INTERNET

The Internet is revolutionising almost every aspect of human endeavour. Areas affected include advertising, entertainment, education, reference material and shopping. The list goes on and on. One of the prime areas it has transformed is travel. Travellers may quickly map out their trip, choosing locations and accommodation after perusing photos or videos, reading online travel magazines or peer reviews, and ultimately booking and paying for flights, car hire and rooms all from the comfort of their living room.

CREATING A WEBSITE

This is for those who may want additional business outside of the reservation platforms. Determine early on the level of involvement you intend to have in creating your site. Are you going to design and create it yourself, or will you pay a professional to create it for you? In either case, the best place to begin is to spend time studying the web, looking at as many sites in the holiday-let/B&B industry as possible and determining what works and what doesn't. When you see a page you like that someone else has created, be sure to note the address and give it to your web designer so that he or she can see the type of design that appeals to you.

Before you can launch a website you will need to purchase and register a *domain name*. The domain name is the name of your site and will cost you a recurring annual fee with the registrar. You also need to choose a web hosting company that will host your website on their servers. Get as much advice and assistance as you require in these early stages. A strong, memorable domain name is crucial, so be deliberate in your choice.

Your web design must reflect your goals, and once those have been identified and an agreed structure is in place, the site design and construction can commence. This process is very different from designing a newspaper advertisement, which can remain static, as it needs to be maintained and updated at regular intervals.

Be sure that you clearly determine the goals of your accommodation site. Is the goal to provide a service, list your property, or to make money or supply some other service?

MILESTONES

In the implementation of your business plan, 'milestones' advise you of your progress. They are proof that the actions you have identified and allocated in your business plan have actually been completed.

Your milestones could be simply:

★ Client list created.
★ Customer survey completed.
★ Analysis mechanism established.
★ Business diary created.
★ Promotional brochure printed.
★ Website completed.
★ Connection of high-speed data access for PC is completed.

Due to the fact that each strategy can entail a large number of actions, you will need a worksheet that lists all the steps and milestones you hope to achieve. This checklist can subsequently be adjusted as required.

ANECDOTE: Running any small accommodation is, for the most part, a personal experience. You are more likely to get a hug from a guest when they depart from your holiday-let/B&B than if you were the manager of a hotel. This has been the experience of many hosts I have encountered at holiday-let/B&B networking meetings and at conferences.

MANAGING CUSTOMER CONTACT

If you manage contact with your customers really well, you need never have difficult guests; you can learn to deal with almost any behaviour type effectively. There are many styles of people management and many situations to be aware of.

Some people's behaviour may be affected by problems they have brought with them. Others will perceive problems in a given situation that you have not even considered. However well you manage your business, you will find yourself dealing with the occasional person with problems.

Building Rapport

One method that has proved to be highly effective in managing people and situations is that of building rapport.

Build rapport with each guest, taking the time to find out how each needs to be treated, how much conversation they prefer to have with you, how much attention they would like.

It isn't about how you like to relate; it's about how your guest needs to relate. You have to put yourself in their shoes.

If you are naturally an extrovert, friendly and outgoing, and enjoy most of your contacts with people, you have to assess whether your guest is also as outgoing.

An introverted guest will not wish to share a great deal of information, or even to spend much time with you.

When an extrovert shares too much information and energy with an introvert, the introvert becomes nervous about how much they are expected to share in return. It's not comfortable for them and you need to be sensitive to their needs. It's best to start out being friendly, but not effusive, and allow your guest to set the level of interaction.

On the other hand, if you are an introvert, you will be comfortable giving other introverts the space they need. You may find extrovert guests a bit of a trial and may need to set personal limits – for example, time constraints – in order to handle them in a friendly and professional manner. If your partner is your opposite in personality type, you may be able to share the guests accordingly, and thus avoid the stresses that can occur.

Small, hosted accommodation enterprises are not just about enjoying social contact with your guests, but about taking care of their needs in an unobtrusive way.

You can ask the usual questions about guests' needs. How do they feel? Do they need more information? Is their room to their liking? If you have set a high and professional standard, most people will be quite happy with such questions, and extroverts will have no hesitation in making any suggestion that they feel is relevant.

Keep in mind that the less extroverted will feel uncomfortable letting you know if anything is wrong and will need a truly accessible way to approach you about any concerns they have. You can provide a written feedback form – with a very simple layout and only a few questions. Or a whiteboard can be provided in the hallway, with a pen of course! And the heading: 'Any Suggestions?'

You can bypass potential trouble spots by asking guests to let you know if there is anything else you can help them with.

The complaints procedure has to be easy to use. Remember, you do want to know if there are any problems.

Problems will occur when your guests behave in a way you didn't expect, or don't welcome, or when what is said is misinterpreted or misunderstood.

You will have an uncomfortable time running your holiday let, Bed and Breakfast or guesthouse if you find it hard to set limits and to let your guests know in a clear way what behaviour is acceptable and what is not.

There have to be limits, and they will vary from place to place. One thing you can't assume is that people will know the rules.

You can have a list of guest expectations placed in the rooms, or in a prominent place in the entry area. In the room is often more effective because guests can take their time to absorb the information, rather than trying to take it in when you are greeting them. This method is especially good for routine matters such as where one can and cannot smoke, or what to do with the rubbish. Areas of difficulty may arise over issues such as how much noise is reasonable, especially where children are involved.

You will need to be assertive at times, and to set limits in a way that feels comfortable for you and your guests.

Epilogue: For the Future

This book has given you an insight into how to run a holiday let/B&B. It is a beginner's introduction into this sector of the accommodation industry. It has never been easier to become a provider of this type of accommodation and to run successfully.

The extraordinary growth of global online reservation platforms and the ease with which you can list your property with them means that you can enter this sector of the accommodation industry with very little capital outlay.

If you already have a suitable property you will need only a relatively small amount of money to cover the cost of getting your property ready for holiday accommodation, as outlined in this book. The financial situation is obviously different if you need to purchase a property.

You don't need a large amount of start-up capital to market your venture, as the reservation platforms do this for you.

As things currently stand, the vast majority of properties listed on online reservation platforms do not comply with local government rules and regulations as they currently apply to existing Bed and Breakfasts; new rules will no doubt soon be established and enforced. For example: fire safety rules that include the provision of smoke detectors in guestrooms and hallways and a fire extinguisher and fire blanket close to the kitchen area.

In many places, local government authorities have changed the rules to allow properties listed with Airbnb to market their properties outside of normal regulations as they apply to small accommodation providers. For example, some local authorities are no longer requiring potential hosts to lodge development applications to operate as a small accommodation provider. This has huge ramifications for the future of the holiday-let/B&B industry. When companies get as big as Airbnb, they can influence the rules.

Sara Kaine, associate professor at the University of Technology, Sydney, says this kind of growth adds to the challenges faced by new businesses. It takes the sharing economy to areas where regulation is already quite vexed and difficult. You start to have risks that you didn't foresee to begin with. Some people start their business with no foreseeable risks, but then tend to take risks when building the business; for example, it's risky not to incorporate local regulations that may later impact on your property. The point to remember is that you have a legal 'duty of care' while hosting guests. If anything goes wrong – such as someone slipping over in the shower, or a fire in the property damaging guests' effects – the host could be liable.

Several companies are now offering a management service for time-poor hosts that includes supplying cleaners and gardeners, handing over and collecting keys to/from the guest, handling online advertisements and arranging airport transfers. These companies are charging a 20 per cent commission for services rendered.

If you get started in holiday lets/B&B as a beginner and find it an enjoyable and profitable experience, you could take the next step and market your property more extensively in the local marketplace.

Four simple steps to remember when running a holiday let/B&B are:

1   YOU MUST EARN MORE MONEY THEN YOU SPEND.
2   YOU MUST PAY YOUR BILLS ON TIME.
3   YOU MUST LOOK AFTER YOUR GUESTS.
4   YOU NEED TO LOOK AFTER YOURSELF AND YOUR STAFF.

Good luck in your venture.

Index

accommodation cash flow 71
accountants 6, 44
accreditation *see* star grading systems
advertising and promotion 10, 82,
    86–7
Airbnb xi, 1, 2, 4, 9, 23, 25, 26, 28, 35,
    59, 66, 71, 78, 79, 93, 105
  bookings 55, 65, 66
  breakfasts 23, 59
  and local government regulations
    xi
  payment 71
  Private Certification 35
  ratings 78
  references 95
  shared bathrooms 26
alcohol 23, 47
alcohol licence 24, 61
'amenity creep' 22
anti-discrimination legislation 11
apps 100

B&B associations 75, 76
B&B classification 77
banks 44
bathrooms and toilets 26–8
  disabled facilities 26
  en-suite 3, 26
  extras 28
  flooring 26
  power points 27

  safety 27, 54
  shared 26
  showers 27
  spa baths 26, 29
  ventilation 26–7
bedrooms 29–31
  bedside lights 30
  coffee and tea facilities 31
  extras 31
  flooring 30
  furnishings 31
  luggage racks 30
  minimum size requirements
    29
beds 29–30
  bed linen 30
  bedmaking 57
  contract quality 29
  electric blankets 30
  zip-up models 30
board games and cards 22
booking.com xi, 2, 79
bookings 65–6
  reservation chart 65
  reservation diary 54, 65
breakfast 23, 59–61
  basics 59
  breakfast baskets 60–1
  continental breakfast 60
  cooked breakfasts 59–60
  presentation 60

building and development applications *see* planning and building approval
burnout 3
business name 98
  registering 98
business plan 7, 8, 43
  milestones 101
business travellers 5, 9, 10–11
buying an established B&B/holiday let 17–18
  goodwill 17

cancellation policies 48
capital gains tax (CGT) 99
certificate of lawful development 39
Chambers of Commerce 90
children
  guests 12, 48
  host's children 8, 15
china 23–4
cleanliness 25, 56, 72
  see also housekeeping
coasters and tablemats 72
coffee, morning 61
coffee and tea facilities 31
commitment 3–4, 6, 8
communication skills 7
  see also people skills
community organisations 90
company status 98
competition, monitoring 83
complaints 52–3, 103
computer literacy 6
contents insurance 69

contingency plan 7
conversation etiquette 49–50
conversions and renovations 17, 33, 37–8
  time frame 38
corporate market 5, 9, 10–11
crockery 23–4
cutlery 24–5

damage to property 51, 69
debt liability
  company 98
  sole trader 97
deposits 48
destination marketing 76–7, 84
diary 65
dietary requirements 48, 65
dining rooms 23–5
dinner 23, 62
direct mail campaigns 90
disabilities, people with 11–12, 48
  bathroom and toilet facilities 26
dishwasher 25–6
'Do not disturb' signs 50
domain name 100–1

eating with guests 62
electric blankets 30
employees 8, 83
employers liability insurance 69
en-suite accommodation 3, 26
entertainment facilities 22
entrance 20–1
Expedia xi, 2
exterior, property 19–20

Facebook 86
failure, reasons for 3
family annexe 8, 15
family life 15
  privacy 15, 21
  separation from work 6, 8, 15
family market 12
farmstays 12, 77, 85
feasibility study 3, 6–7, 8, 79
feedback 52, 53, 103
finance 43, 44
financial advisors 18, 42, 43, 70, 97,
    98
financial goals 6–7
financial model 79–80
financial records 70–1
  market research and 83–4
financial software 6, 70
fire blankets 36
fire safety 34, 36–7, 54–5, 105
first aid 56–7
first impressions 19–20
flooring
  bathrooms and toilets 26
  bedrooms 30
  kitchen 25
  porch and hallway 21
flowers, fresh 28
food poisoning 55
food preparation and storage 54, 55–6
  critical control points (CCPs) 56
  hazards 56
food safety legislation 25, 34
food-handling courses 55
foreign currency payments 71
Four in a Bed (TV series) 87

'freebies' 10, 89
furnishings 23, 37–8
  care of 72–3

garden furniture 20
garden maintenance 20, 73
gay community 11
glassware 24
goals 6–7
goodwill 17
grading systems *see* star grading
    systems
GST/VAT 99
guest registration 66–7
  register 67
  registration cards 67
guesthouse classification 77
guests
  behaviour 7, 50–1
  comments and suggestions 82–3,
      103
  complaints 52–3, 103
  initial slow flow of 7
  managing customer contact 49–53,
      102–3
  questionnaires 53
  rapport, building 102–3
  reasons for staying in a holiday
      let/B&B 5, 87
  references 95
  target market 9–13, 79, 81, 90

heating and cooling 21, 31
Hepatitis B vaccination 55
high tea 61–2
holiday lets 3

home office 31–2

hospitality industry 75–80

hosts

  commitment 3–4, 6, 8

  communication skills 7

  computer literacy 6

  duty of care 34, 106

  people skills 49–53, 102–3

  personality 7

  reasons to enter the short-let and
    B&B market 2–4

  single people 8

  staying in other B&B and holiday
    lets 7

house rules 103

housekeeping 71–2

  checklist 72

  furniture care 72–3

  hygiene 55–6

hygiene practices *see* cleanliness;
    housekeeping

Inland Revenue Office 70

insurance 44, 67–70

  alternative accommodation and rent
    69

  contents cover 69

  Duty of Disclosure 70

  employers liability insurance 69

  product liability insurance 69

  public liability insurance 68–9

Internet 86, 100

kitchen 25–6, 54

  safety 25, 54, 55–6

leaflets 91

legal structure of the business
    97–8

  company 98

  partnership 97–8

  sole trader 97

  trusts 98

letting period, defined 8

lifestyle change 2, 3, 5–6, 16

lighting 19, 20, 73

linen suppliers 30

Lions Club 90

living rooms 21–2

local area information, providing 11,
    13, 48

local government regulations xi, 33–6,
    105

  see also planning and building
    approval

local tourist organisations 76, 90

location 5–6, 16, 18

  busy tourist areas 16

  city suburbs 16

  country towns 16

locks

  bathrooms 27

  bedrooms 31

  and fire safety 54

lounges, guest 21–2

luggage racks 30

lunch 61

maintenance 19–20

management services 106

market research 9–10, 81–4

  competition 83

employee contributions
83
guest comments and suggestions
82–3
records and files 83–4
marketing 81–91
budget 90–1
expenses 89
marketing concept 81
marketing mix 81, 86
marketing plan 90–1
marketing strategy 81, 84–5
target marketing 85–6
see also advertising and promotion;
public relations
meals
eating with guests 62
see also breakfast; dinner; lunch
media kits 88, 89
mentors 43, 45
midweek stays 5, 86, 91

neighbours 51–2
networking 45, 75
newsletters 53, 90, 91
niche markets 10, 12
non-smoking policy 12, 48

occupancy rates 79–80
onefinestay 2
online reservation platforms xi, 1–2,
4, 10, 34, 93–5
apps 100
commission structures 95
fees 95
guest ratings 95

local authority regulations 33, 34,
35
management services 106
payments 95
property listings 47–8, 94
property owners, risks for 93
property ratings 53, 95
regulation 93, 105
see also individual platforms
open fires 22
over-capitalisation 3
overseas travellers 10, 26, 62, 67

partnership 97–8
Partnership Agreement 97–8
passports 67
payment 71, 95
people skills 49–53, 102–3
pets 12–13, 48, 54
catering for 13
picnic baskets 61
planning and building approval 33–4,
35, 38–9
planning and preparation 41–5
business plan 7, 8, 43
feasibility study 3, 6–7, 8, 79
finance 43
professional support 43–5
self-questionnaire 42–3
popularity of the B&B/holiday-let
industry 5
power boards 31
power points 27, 30–1
press releases 88–9
media kits 88, 89
targeting your story 88–9

privacy 15, 21
  guests 49, 50, 62
Private Certification 35
product differentiation 86
product liability insurance 69
professional support 43–5
professionalism xii
property
  buying an established B&B/holiday
    let 17–18
  conversion 17, 33, 37–8
  custom building 17
  first impressions 19–20
  location 5–6, 16, 18
  potential 16–17, 37
  preparation 19–32
  viability 33
  your existing property 15–16
public liability insurance 68–9
public relations 87–9, 90
  press releases 88–9

ratings 78
  online reservation platforms 53,
    95
  see also star grading systems
reasons to enter the short-let and
    B&B market 2–4
registration see guest registration
repeat business 17
reservation chart 65
reservation diary 54, 65
restaurant recommendations 48,
    62–3
room rates
  displaying 99

factors affecting 60, 99
flexible pricing policy 84, 91
setting 98–9
Rotary Club 90

safety 54–5
  bathroom 27, 54
  cleaning duties 55
  duty of care 34
  fire safety 34, 36–7, 54–5, 105
  first aid 56–7
  food handling and storage 25, 34,
    55–6
  kitchen 25, 54, 55–6
seasonality 16, 17
seed capital 43
self-contained accommodation 3, 12,
    16, 62, 77
  breakfast baskets 60–1
sharing economy xi, 1–2, 34, 35, 93,
    106
  see also online reservation platforms
sharing your home 8, 15, 21
short-break holiday market xi, 4, 5
showers 27
signage 19, 20
single travellers 11
smartphones 100
smoke alarms 36
smoking 12, 48
social media 86
sole trader 97
solicitors 44, 97, 98
spa baths 26, 29
special interest tourism 10
  see also destination marketing

special offers 91
star grading systems 77–8
  statutory obligations 77
surveys 37, 38

table linen 24
target market 9–13, 79, 81, 90
target marketing 85–6
  demographic segment 85
  geographic segment 85
  previous guests 85
  product benefits 85
  special interest groups 85
tax 31–2, 44, 70, 89
  capital gains tax (CGT) 99
  companies 98
  GST/VAT 70, 99
  sole traders 97
tea, afternoon 49, 61–2
televisions 22
toilet paper 28
toiletries 28
toilets *see* bathrooms and toilets

tourism authorities 4, 45, 75–6
tourism trends 4, 82
tourist information centres 9
towels 28
trade discounts 29
trade and tourism shows 90
TripAdvisor xi, 1, 2, 4, 79, 87, 93
trusts 98
turnover 80
Twitter 86

Uber xi
university and college visitors 10

VAT/GST records 70
views 22–3, 84

website, building a 100–1
welcoming guests 21, 49, 61
Wimdu xi, 1, 4, 79, 93
women travellers 11
word-of-mouth recommendations
    7, 11, 87, 89, 90, 95